FOREVER NEWLYWEDS

Secrets to Creating and Growing Passion in Your
Relationship That Lasts Forever

Keven & Marianne Card

Published by Storehouse Publishing Houston, TX.

This title may be purchased in bulk for educational, business, fund-raising, or sales promotional use. For information please email: forevernewlyweds@live.com

CONTENTS

Acknowledgements

Most importantly, we want to thank God for always watching out for us and giving us hope when we needed it most. We dedicate this book to God because without Him this wouldn't have ever been possible.

I would also like to thank my wife, who has inspired my life so dramatically that I have been able to overcome so many things. She is my pillar to lean on. She is truly my guardian angel; I love you, honey, with everything that I am.

We'd like to thank our children, Stephanie and Branden, who are incredible children and have made us the most blessed parents in the world. We are proud of what you both have become, we love you both will all our hearts.

We want to thank some very special people who have been a significant inspiration which allowed us to complete this book: Denise Caldwell, who doesn't even know the significance of her role in why we wrote this book. Mike and Fiona Mellett and all the Lakewood Church Choir members, you are our extended family; Pastor Joel and Victoria Osteen, who, without even knowing, reminded us that with God on your side anything is possible and helped us to have enough faith to step out of our box and let God take us to new places.

Introduction

Life is such an amazing experience. It has its ups and its downs, its victories and its defeats. But most of all, we are rarely, if ever, fully prepared for what life has in store for us. In the area of our marriages this has never been truer. Marriage can be a richly rewarding experience, or it can be tragic and disastrous one. To see the difference, just watch how couples are with each other the next time you're in a restaurant.

Some couples are just enjoying each other and carrying on a lively conversation, but often we see couples who are just the opposite. They are together, but it seems as if they would rather be anywhere else but sitting with their spouse, eating a meal. They sit in complete silence. One may be reading the newspaper while the other slowly eats. No words are exchanged and they hardly look at each other. It's almost like they are in an awkward situation or something, and before they are finished chewing the last bite of food, one of them will stand up and leave. You can see the reluctance to even say goodbye to each other. It makes you wonder what happened between them. I mean, what was so terrible that they can't even eat a meal together?

The question is how can we avoid ending up like that? What can we do to make our marriage go all the way? What is it that some couples have, that others don't?

We know that nearly all couples basically start out the same. We start out in love and happy, we want to do things for our girlfriend or boyfriend that pleases them, and we begin to develop a connection. One day we decide that we love this person; so much so that we can't live without them. We want to spend the rest of our life with this one person.

We do this without any real thought to what it means to be married or the real commitment that it takes. We just think to ourselves, "I love this person and I love being with this person. I want to spend the rest of my life with this person." We don't really care to know how many kids we'll have, what kind of job we'll need to support our family, or where we'll live. We don't even care to find out how much the wedding will actually cost or who will pay for it. We just know that we want to be with that person and no one else. And then we make that all important decision to get married and start our lives together.

We also know that most couples believe that they can stand the test of time. Couples often respond when asked the question, "What if your marriage doesn't last?" They'll say something similar to "Our marriage will last because we're in love," or "We're different because we understand each other." Even in the wedding vows we say to each other "till death do us part" without any thought to how long that may actually be. We just know that this person is the one and we're not going to let anyone change our minds. We just step out in faith and believe that we will and can finish the race together.

So if we want to start our lives together and we want to finish together, then why are so many relationships falling apart? Do they decide that they no longer want to be together? Or does it just happen slowly? Even the ones who stay together, it's as if they are living with a roommate instead of their spouse, in a constant struggle that develops into a love/hate relationship. How and when does this happen?

The answer is what happens in the middle, the time between when we start together and when we finish together. We have to grow up together and learn how to become a couple. We must reach the conclusion that our relationship is the most valuable possession that we have in this life; it is a treasure and it is what makes us rich. We have to build a bond strong enough to weather any of the storms that will come. A bond that is built through overcoming adversity; we must be willing to fight for each other, not with each other. This growing up together part *is* the test; it is when we find out what we are truly made of. It determines if we will rise above the world's view of a life together, or will we become just another victim of statistics?

We want to show you a new vision, a vision where you start to live the good life. The one where being happy together is not only in the beginning, but can also be throughout the life of your marriage, *and* at the end of your life. We want to show you how to make happiness a lifestyle. We want you to experience to true wealth and live a fulfilling life together, to have the endurance to overcome challenges in this lifetime. We want to help you unlock the true potential of your relationship, and teach you how valuable your spouse or significant other really is. We want to show you how to develop a foundation in your relationship that is based on the real meaning of love. We want you to have a connection that is unbreakable and know that your marriage can be the one that walks into the sunset and lives happily-ever-after.

Chapter 1

What is a Rich Life?

Proverbs 13:7 (NKJV): There is one who makes himself rich, yet has nothing; and one who makes himself poor, yet has great wealth.

There are two definitions of rich: the first is various ways of saying that you have a lot of money or own expensive property. But, did you know that you can be rich and yet have nothing in the way of possessions or money? You can also have accumulated great amounts of money and have many possessions only to be completely miserable. All you have to do to know this is true is to look at the news about famous Hollywood actors that so many of us revere and admire. How often do we hear news of celebrity marriages falling apart, followed by bitter divorces? Or that an unfortunate overdose caused the death of a famed actor or actress?

They have plenty of wealth and possessions, so why are they so unhappy? Why are so many of the people that we "look up to" in society as messed up or more messed up in their personal lives than we are? The answer for most of us, as unbelievable as it sounds is, that material wealth is not what makes anyone happy, nor does it give one a sense of fulfillment. We believe that *"rich"* means having something of great value to you, something you cherish. There is only one

1

thing that people can have in this lifetime that can make them truly rich and it's not money or possessions; it is a loving family; it's through sharing their lives with someone they love and can enjoy being with. To go to bed each night and wake up each day next to someone who makes them smile just because they're together.

It's a great spouse that makes us rich because we find true happiness just in being with that one person that we can love for the rest of our life.

Proverbs 19: 14 House and land are handed down from parents, but a congenial spouse comes straight from God.

If you search your heart, we believe that you'll come to the same conclusion that we have: That money and possessions are not the riches that we truly desire for our lives. The treasure that we all seek is to love and to be loved. When you truly give your heart away to your spouse and they give their heart to you, you hold each others lives in your hands, and *that* is a true treasure.

What treasure out there could be more valuable than the one that can love us even when we can't love ourselves; to help us get back up when we fail at a great business idea or get fired from a job; to take care of us when we're sick; and give us an encouraging word when the storms, that so often come in life, are battering on top of us? That is a treasure that is priceless and irreplaceable, a treasure that you should want to keep very close to you so it will not lose any of its value. That treasure should be so valuable that you would protect it with your life.

Your treasure is your spouse and you are their treasure. Your treasure box is your marriage and there is **nothing** that will give your life more meaning and more pleasure than a great spouse and a happy and rewarding marriage.

Proverbs 31: 10-11 (Message): A good woman is hard to find, and worth far more than diamonds. Her husband trusts her without reserve, and never has reason to regret it.

My treasure is my wife! I admit right now that I am guilty of loving my wife so deeply that I can not adequately express my deepest feelings for her. The words "I love you" just seem to be too small for what I really want to communicate to her, each and every day that I wake up and look her in the eyes.

I am one of those husbands that does say "I love you" at least ten times a day (and that's on a bad day). I say "I love you" before I get off the phone with her and if I didn't hear her say "I love you" back to me, I call her right back and make sure that she heard me say those words and I heard her say them. I am guilty of kissing my wife in public so much that people tend to think that we are newlyweds.

We hold hands everywhere we go, even when no one is around. I am guilty of opening doors for my wife so that she doesn't have to. Admittedly, I make breakfast for her every

3

Saturday and Sunday morning so that she can sleep in. I have been known to show up unexpectedly at her work with flowers or to surprise her and take her out for a romantic dinner for two. I am guilty of being a husband who wants to see his wife happy all the time. The amazing thing about being willing to meet my wife's needs is that in turn she is willing to meet my needs.

Proverbs 18:22 (Message): Find a good spouse and find a good life-and even more: the favor of God!

My wife is guilty of loving me so much that she tells me "I love you" at least ten times a day. She holds my hand everywhere we go. She always saves the last piece of whatever we are eating for me. She always shares her drinks with me.

She calls me from work just to tell me that she's thinking about me and how much she misses me and, of course, that she loves me too. She always laughs at my jokes even when they're not funny. She always tells me how she is proud of me even when I am not proud of myself. She even makes love to me when she is tired and doesn't really want to and she never has a headache at the wrong time. She goes out of her way to make sure I am happy.

The bottom line is that when you're living a rich married life, you're both happy nearly all the time. The thought never crosses your mind that you would ever leave your spouse, because you feel complete. Having a rich marriage is not about having an abundance of money, but rather an abundance of love and happiness, just being with your spouse. When your needs are being met by your spouse and their needs are being met by you, that's the good life. Some of the happiest couples we know have very little in the way of money or possessions but they have love and lots of it.

My wife is originally from the Philippines and she has quite a few family members who still live there who have not been blessed with an abundance of money. But, what I can tell you about them is that they enjoy their lives and they love each other more than most people will ever love each other.

In some cases they must leave their family to go overseas just to find work, to make any money at all. They often will only see each other once per year; some as few as once every three years. What I found amazing about that is how they still remain so dedicated and faithful to each other even under those circumstances. They love each other and it shows in the way they talk and the way they act. That's what we believe love should be and is the foundation that we have built our own relationship on.

More importantly, the love they share not only affects their lives but their children's lives as well. You see when couples are living a rich married life, where love is the theme of their relationship; it can't help but to spill over into the lives of their children.

I don't say this arrogantly, but we often have complete strangers walk up to us and tell us how great our children are, how respectful and helpful they are. They are like that not because we did anything special, but because my wife and I share a deep and unbreakable love for each other that spills over into their lives and makes them feel loved. That fills their lives with love and that love spills over; then they are able to go out and show love to the world around them because they have extra that they can give away.

It seems to us that that's the way God intended it to be and we're certain that you would agree. We're here to tell you that there is nothing in this world more valuable in this lifetime than your family. They are priceless and they are irreplaceable and they should be second only to a personal relationship with God.

I was home one day, we were spending time together as a family, and I'll never forget how powerful this day was for me: That day my son, Branden, looked up at me and with the most sincere voice I have ever heard him speak, he said, "Dad, you're my best friend and I love you." Those words pierced my heart and melted me, I've never admitted this before, but later on when I was alone and I was thinking about that day, I cried, because at that moment I realized that I was loved and I don't mean one of those 'I love you because I have to' kind of loves. I mean truly loved. I am loved by my wife, my daughter, and my son and I felt (and still do feel) like the richest man alive. You see when you are living a rich married life, you come to realize that what makes you happy doesn't matter, but it's what you do for God, then your spouse, then your children, then your friends, your job and then yourself.

The kind of life that you've been searching for all your life is about what you do for others and not about what others do for you. God will take care of you when you selflessly take care of the people in your life.

You can have a rich married life and you can start to build it right now. No matter how good or bad your current marriage is, the tools that we'll share with you can help you to begin the process of healing and delivering your marriage from anything that is holding you back from having the rich marriage that you deserve.

We want to give you the hope you've been searching for and we want you to know that whatever you are going through right now, we understand, and we can tell you that you are not alone. God knows that you have been trying to work things out but you haven't found the answers that you have been looking for that can help you turn it around.

Well, we want to say to you right now that today is a new day and we believe that if you are reading this book it's because we prayed for the people who needed this book to find it and we believe that's you; so we encourage you to embrace this day as a day when anything can happen and will happen.

We declare right now that you'll find your rich married life waiting for you within these pages. We may not know your name, but please know that we are praying for you and your marriage every single day.

Chapter 2

Becoming a Couple

In order to find a forever-kind-of-love, you must first understand what it means to be married and how you grow together. You see, when you're dating, everything just seems to fit into its place just right. Your boyfriend or girlfriend seems to want to give you exactly what you need and even what you want, showering you with affection, buying you gifts, giving you his/her undivided attention, and taking you anywhere you want to go. So, the real question isn't whether or not you can meet each other's needs, but rather why the focus has changed. We believe the answer to that question can be found in the book of Matthew.

Matthew 19:5 (Message): He answered, "Haven't you read in your Bible that the Creator originally made man and woman for each other, male and female? And because of this, a man leaves father and mother and is firmly bonded to his wife, becoming one flesh—no longer two bodies but one. Because God created this organic union of the two sexes, no one should desecrate his art by cutting them apart."

We believe that when we first begin the courting process that we are two completely separate individuals with our own feelings and emotions. We hold our individuality in high regard because we have developed certain likes and dislikes, beliefs, and characteristics.

Once we marry, then our individuality ceases to exist and "two become one"; however, our individuality is still trying desperately to hold on and it fills us with conflicting feelings and emotions. But because in the beginning we are "in love", we tend to overlook many of the things that our new spouse does that we may not like, or that offend us. Let's face it, at this stage most of us have been single all of our lives and it's a transforming experience for us to have to be accountable to someone else. Unfortunately, once the "in love" experience begins to wear off, we start to express our offenses to each other; that is when love must conquer, because the melding process has now gone into full swing and the battle to become one flesh has begun. We believe that it's through this struggle to become one that we grow to be a strong couple.

You have to think of it this way, a great marriage is much like the making of a great sword. Nearly everyone is amazed by the beauty, sophistication, and deadliness of a well-made sword; but most of us do not know the lengthy process it takes to make such a lethal work of art. It begins with carbon charcoal and iron sand. You combine these two elements by melting them together in a furnace. Once the elements are combined you are left with a block of raw material that hardly resembles a work of art, but more like a mangled lump of metal with an incredible amount of rough edges. Then the metal is put through a process where it's superheated, beaten out, and then suddenly cooled. The amazing thing about this process is that each time the sword is superheated, more of the impurities come out of the metal, making it stronger and stronger.

It is only when nearly all the impurities have been removed and the desired shape has taken form does the sword smith polish his weapon, put the handle on it, and engrave it with the beautiful designs that we often see. Then the sword is filed to make it so sharp that it becomes not only a masterpiece but a deadly weapon as well. However, the unique thing about a sword is that even after it has been masterfully forged and sharpened to perfection, you must grind the blade frequently or it will become dull and it will not be capable of fulfilling its purpose.

The same can be said of marriage. Man and woman are two completely different beings, put together in the process of courtship, and then suddenly fused together in holy matrimony, and most often without fully and completely knowing each other.

In the beginning the newness feels incredible, it's warm and we are getting closer together. However, the closer we get the more we start to see little flaws being exposed. Once the in love experience has ended we become aware of all the rough edges that our relationship has and rough edges can be very unattractive. Then the growing up together process begins and it has the potential to be a very rewarding experience if it is viewed correctly; but we firmly believe that this is the period when many couples' relationship begins to fracture. However, if we want to weather all of these storms, we must learn to allow these processes to purify our relationship, and know that these challenges are only going to make us stronger as a couple and should serve to draw us closer together and never to tear us apart. Every time we overcome one of life's challenges, we become more united, our relationship grows a little stronger, and the more valuable our love becomes.

Our marriages can and should be as valuable to us as a sword is in the hands of a skilled warrior. It should be our focus because we know that it can save us in the midst of a battle. A skilled warrior spends hours sharpening and grooming his sword in preparation for the battle that may never come, but he is always prepared if it does. Like a warrior we must spend the necessary time to sharpen and groom our marriage in preparation for the battles that we will inevitably face in life. There will be enemies that come to try to steal our treasure right out from under us and we must be prepared.

Anyone can enjoy the rich married life if they are willing to do whatever it takes to make the necessary preparations for all the challenges that are ahead of them and to allow the process to bring them closer together, making them united as one, and insulating them against the world that will do everything in its power to tear that unity apart.

If we were to place the equivalent value on our relationship that a warrior did in the making of his sword, then we would focus our energy on making it stronger. Each time we would put our marriages in the furnaces of life we would only see it as a process of strengthening our relationship and developing a marriage that can withstand the battles that every marriage will face. Our relationship is our sword and if we take care of it, it will serve us well as a weapon and when it becomes an antique it will be admired by all who see it.

The 1ˢᵗ Key

Live to Give,

Not to Get

Chapter 3

How to Get What You Want From Them

I read a story recently about a husband who was massaging his wife's feet, which I love to do for my wife from time to time; but this was the third hour of rubbing his wife's feet when he had a thought – "wouldn't it be great if someone else were doing this?" But instead of just thinking it, he actually said it.

The fight was on. Suddenly she leaped from the couch and flopped down in the recliner; snatching the remote, she changed the channel from the baseball game (that he was watching) to a house remodeling show. Then the silent treatment began. Seeing that his wife was "unjustly" mad, he decided that two can play at that game and in retaliation, began his own silent treatment by reading the newspaper.

A short while later, the wife was the one to raise the white flag first; she changed the channel back and went to him apologizing. Instead of focusing his attention on her apologizing to him, he decided that he could listen to her say she was sorry at the same time he watched the baseball game! When his wife said to him "You don't want to kiss me?" he replies, "When the weather comes on." Needless to say, that rekindled the argument and the fight was back on.

It wasn't until he remembered that he was the needy one and that she went out of her way for him, laughing at his jokes, holding his hand whenever they went out, that he realized that he was the one being ridiculous and needed to make things right; so he finally made up with his wife after hours of things being ugly between them.

I am certain some variant of this story has been played out in the lives of every couple. We get caught up in this idea of "what have you done for me lately." The fact is that we all want our needs to be met by our spouses. We need them to fulfill us emotionally, physically, and intellectually. When we need to hear "I love you," they should be willing to jump up and say, "I love you"; or when we need them to be a little romantic, then they should turn into Casanova. If we need a hug, we should be able to go to them and find one. Of course, elected most important, when we need to express ourselves, they should take the time to listen to what we have to say and understand and accept that it's our point of view, even when they disagree; to be considerate and kind to us; and to love us, especially when we make mistakes.

Acts 20:35 (Message): You'll not likely go wrong here if you keep remembering that our Master said, 'You're far happier giving than getting.'"

The funny thing is that most of us walk around saying, "if my spouse would just do this then I could be happy" or "if they would just stop doing that then I would feel loved." When the truth is that even if your spouse did everything you ever wanted, you would still feel incomplete and unhappy because love is something we give away and not something that we take. Being rich is about loving your spouse enough to want to give them what they need without any strings attached other than the faith that God will give you what you need. It is in what we give to our spouses that gives us our value and makes us complete.

A. Husbands

*Ephesians 5: 25-28 (Message) Husbands, go all out in your love for your wives, exactly as Christ did for the church—**a love marked by giving, not getting**. Christ's love makes the church whole. His words evoke her beauty. Everything he does and says is designed to bring the best out of her, dressing her in dazzling white silk, radiant with holiness. And that is how husbands ought to love their wives. They're really doing themselves a favor—since they're already "one" in marriage.*

Ladies, don't get too excited yet because the bible doesn't say that your husband should run out and buy you gifts- a happy marriage is not about material things, it's about love, honor and respect; sacrificing one's self and one's needs to satisfy the other's needs. It's about doing the right thing or saying the right thing in order to encourage and build the other up and never to tear them down.

17

A husband's love should be so deep for his wife that anything he ever does, he will first take into consideration what the impact on his wife would be. God has called husbands to love and cherish their wives in the same way that Christ loves the church, and that's an amazing love. Just think about it, Christ died for the church (we are the church). He gave the ultimate sacrifice for his bride so that we could be set free from the bondages of this world and have an abundant life.

The responsibility of developing a rich and fulfilling marriage does not just lie on the shoulders of husbands; wives have a responsibility to support their husbands and to help them find happiness. It is only when the husband focuses all of his energy on fulfilling the needs of his wife, and the wife focuses all her attention on fulfilling her husband's needs, that you will find a truly rich marriage.

The world says that a marriage is fifty/fifty; but *we* say that a rich marriage is when the husband gives his wife one-hundred and ten percent and the wife gives her husband one-hundred and ten percent. When we can achieve that, then we know without a doubt that we are blessed, and nothing that's thrown at us will ever be able to separate the bond between us. That's when you know you can withstand the test of time and love each other for the rest of your days.

No person was ever honored for what he received.
Honor has been the reward for what he gave.
-- Calvin Coolidge, American President

B. Wives

Ephesians 5:22-24 (Message) Wives, understand and support your husbands in ways that show your support for Christ. The husband provides leadership to his wife the way Christ does to his church, not by domineering but by cherishing. So just as the church submits to Christ as he exercises such leadership, wives should likewise submit to their husbands.

We know that the idea of this one word "submit" makes most people cringe, but allow us to give you an alternative perspective. It is clearly defined in the Bible that marriage is when two become one. If you are one-half of a whole, then it's no different than being right-or left-handed, one has to be the lead hand. That does not diminish in any way the importance of the other hand because without two hands our abilities would be more than limited. So really, each is as important as the other; it is merely who is responsible as the leader when we have to stand before God and give an account of our lives.

However, think about this for one second; if the husband is following God's word and loving his wife in a way that is marked by giving and not getting, and he is fulfilling the needs of his wife; in turn, a wife honoring God's word loves and respects her husband and fulfills the needs of her husband; then wouldn't it be true that they are both fulfilled and therefore happy?

A truly rich marriage is about serving each other's needs; and it is when we step out in faith, through serving, that God makes sure that all of our needs are met. You see if we focus, not on what **we** want or what **we** need, but what our spouses want and what they need and they in turn focus their attention on meeting our needs, what happens is that everyone is walking in love which is what we are called to do according to The Word and that makes God happy. Now everyone is happy. God is happy because we are walking in love; you're happy because you feel loved and your needs are met; and your spouse is happy because they are loved and their needs are being met.

Better yet, the side effect of a loving relationship is that everyone feels loved and you end up so happy and so loved that it will spill over into others lives, like your children, your parents, and others. Anyone and everyone who comes within five feet of you will see love bubbling off of you like a glowing light around you; and you can let the light of your marriage shine for the world to see; and you mark my words, your light can shine for others and it will help them find their way.

Do you want to know how powerful this vision could be? We can change the world one family at a time if we can get the world to see that true wealth already lives in their home and that they go to bed next to their treasure each night and wake up next to it each morning. If we can inject happiness into the family and heal that family, then we can heal the neighborhoods. If we can heal the neighborhoods, then we can heal a block. If we can heal a block, then we can heal an entire city. If we can heal a city, then we can heal the whole state. If we can heal a state, then we can heal an entire country. Praise God, if we can heal a country, then we can heal the vast world that we live in. What an amazing thought.

Well, you say, "It can't possibly be that simple." How would you ever know unless you're willing to do what we are suggesting and see this vision in action for yourself? We are here to tell you, that it is that simple, and we have done it in our own marriage. If we can do it then anyone can do it. If what we are saying could change everything you don't like about your marriage, and put you on the road to a loving, caring, and fulfilling relationship with your spouse, wouldn't it be worth it to find out? The fact is, this concept is in line with the overall theme of the Bible which is summed up in Matthew.

Matthew 7:12(Message) Here is a simple, rule-of-thumb guide for behavior: Ask yourself what you want people to do for you, then grab the initiative and do it for them. Add up God's Law and Prophets and this is what you get.

It is really quite simple if you think about it. It's all about the "Golden Rule," do unto others as you would have them do unto you. Here's the catch: it starts with you and not your spouse. If you were to go to them first and say, "I'm not happy and you have to start treating me this way!" they would likely get offended and just pull away from you. Once they're offended, they would probably tell you what they don't like about you in as an obnoxious way as they could muster up; then you would get offended; and then everyone is unhappy. One or the other of you must take the first step and stop waiting for the other to do it first.

You will never find happiness in waiting for others to take the first step because, guess what, they're waiting for you to take the first step. If no one is willing to take the initiative, then everyone remains in the same unhappy situation, which leads to misery because nobody's needs are being met. Sounds like pure insanity to us and I hope it does to you as well. Instead of all that, why not lean on God and have a little faith that when you do the right thing, God will give you what He promised.

Psalm 37:4 (NIV): Delight yourself in the LORD and he will give you the desires of your heart.

If it's your desire to have a rich and fulfilled married life, then God promises that if you delight in Him then He will give you that desire; but you have to delight in him first. Obeying God simply means that we trust Him to know what's best for us. We must understand that God's plan for our marriage is bigger and better than any that we could ever possibly dream up for ourselves. If you give your cares to Him and focus on what you do and not on what your spouse does, you'll begin to see happiness start to enter into your life.

Even in our own marriage we had to come to a point where we had to make a decision to focus on each other and what the other needed instead of what we wanted. I'll never forget the very first time in our marriage I asked my wife, "What do you need from me in order to be happy?" and I told her that I would do my best to give her what she needed. Of course, I had already told her what I needed to be happy (I was still figuring this all out at the time, so give me a little bit of a break).

The point is we agreed to focus on each other. I do what I can for my wife to make her happy in our marriage and she does what she can to help make me happy. And I am here to tell you that we have lived up to that vow to each other; and although we have seen some very difficult times, we have survived every one of them. We are also living the rich married life that we are sharing with you in the hope that you can find the happiness that we share.

When you accept this concept as true and you start to focus on what you can give instead of what you can get, you'll have more love in your marriage, you'll have more happiness in your home, and you will set yourself free from all the pain that comes with a divided family. When you start giving selflessly, you'll have found the first key to having a deeper, more fulfilling relationship with your spouse.

The 2nd Key

Get Rid of Oversized Expectations and Misconceptions

Chapter 4

Get Rid of Oversized Expectations

A couple of weekends ago, my wife and I facilitated at a married life event that we have at our church and the subject of expectations came up. One of the wives there made the point that she doesn't expect anything from her husband; her rationale was that it was because we can only expect things from ourselves and not from others. Her heart was in the right place, that we can't have oversized expectations from our mate, but we all have expectations. I gently explained to her that she does expect her husband to love her, provide for her, take time to listen to her, and commit to his marriage vows; and that those are expectations, but completely reasonable ones. It's when we allow our expectations to get oversized that we start to see some complications.

When we are growing up, we all develop ideas of what a good marriage looks like. We may have seen what a good marriage is from an example set by our own parents or grandparents. Or maybe an aunt or uncle's marriage was the example. There are those of us who didn't have good examples in our own family; perhaps we knew of a family down the street and wished our family was more like them. Still others of us got our example from watching movies.

The point is that we all have some ideas of what we expected when we got married. Very often though, the ideas we have come from more of a dream or a wish they from a realistic point of view. Why? Because when we're young we don't have the right perspective to understand all the work that is required to be married.

Far too many have found out that after the wedding bells have been silenced, life takes a twist of events that we didn't prepare for, and we start to slowly sink from our high perch in the clouds. The primary reason begins with our expectations of what marriage should be.

Women often fall into the dream of the happily-ever-after marriage. You know the one, where the Prince and the Princess get married and ride off into the sunset and they are just happy; nothing bad ever happens to them. They dream of a husband who loves everything about them and never disagrees with them; they sing and dance together in front of a fireplace after taking an extended vacation to a faraway place. Often her dream husband is handsome, wealthy, has straight, pearly white teeth, and gives her whatever her heart desires.

Men, on the other hand, often dream of a wife who likes to do the same things they do, watch the game, go fishing, or hang out on the couch. He wants her to have dinner ready for him when he gets home from a hard day at work; and she is ready to pamper him for being such a good provider for the family.

The expectations of what the other should and shouldn't do are already so high when we get married, that when our spouses are not living up to our initial expectations we start to get discouraged. When we are discouraged for too long, then feelings that our spouse no longer cares about us develop. Because they're not meeting our needs, eventually resentment sets in, and once that takes root, then unhappiness and misery soon follow. We're left wondering what happened, it's as if the unhappiness just snuck up on us and hit us in the face and we are left stunned.

The goods news is that you don't have to remain unhappy in your marriage (no we are not telling you to run and get a divorce; you wouldn't be any happier even if you did). We want to give you the tools that you need to be the way you and your spouse were when you were dating, or even better than you were. We want you to *live* life; have a rich marriage, living happy and free from the torments that most marriages experience today. It all begins with understanding some of the misconceptions that are embedded in our minds about marriage and our relationships, and then getting rid of those oversized expectations and setting ourselves free.

Chapter 5

In Love vs. Love

"Love" is such a special word that is, at its core, the very reason that we exist. If it were not for love, God himself would have had no reason to create the wonders of life that we take for granted each and every day. Take just one moment right now and look out your window, or, if you're reading this at night, go outside right now and look up at the sky, and just for a moment, ask why were we put here? Ask yourself, why would God take the time to create such a wondrous place? We believe that He created this miracle so He could enjoy a relationship with you, the same way that a father would enjoy the relationship with his own son or daughter.

The unfortunate reality is that we often misuse the word love. Far too often we use this word to describe simple pleasures such as "I love shopping" or "I love baseball" when the reality is that we enjoy those things greatly, but truthfully we do not love them. We also tend to misunderstand the difference between the "in love" experiences of our relationships and what love truly is.

I'll never forget the day that I met my wife because it was the day that changed my life forever. It was November 2, 1991 and I had just walked into the best disco in Guam, the Onyx Night Club. I was walking along the walkway that paralleled the dance floor, when this brilliant smile caught the corner of my eye. As I looked over, our eyes met, and right then it was as if all of the blood in my body suddenly rushed to my face. I could actually feel the heat that blushing created. Embarrassed, I broke eye contact, and trying not to seem obvious, I practically ran up the stairs to the second floor. I couldn't believe how strangely I was acting. I mean I had been to that club probably hundreds of times and I had met my share of women, but I never, ever felt the way that I felt that night. I just knew I had to meet her; but this time, I had no idea what I was going to do.

Standing on the second-floor catwalk, on the opposite side of the club, I stood there just staring at her, trying to come up with a good plan to approach her; when she looked up and saw me staring, embarrassment number two. Now I was really rattled. All these thoughts started swimming around in my head; I kept thinking that she probably thought I was some freak who only liked to stare. So I went back downstairs to the bar and ordered a drink. As I was ordering, this girl standing next to me started talking to me and asking me questions. I explained my predicament and it turned out that this girl knew the woman that I couldn't bring *myself* to talk to.

I talked with her for a little while, really just sizing up how I could get this girl to do me a favor and find out if I could meet this incredible woman that I was now in fear of. I finally succeeded and I convinced her to get permission from my future wife to come meet her and sit with her. I walk up to Marianne and the second our hands met I was in love and all I knew was that I wanted to be with her the rest of my life. I didn't know it at the time, but that was the night my life changed because I had met my wife.

Now that I have told you more than I probably should have about how I met my wife, let me share an important secret with you. Though it is absolutely true that at that point I was "in love" with my wife; and as a matter of fact, within a couple of months I proposed marriage to her; there was not any love in our relationship. Now wait, don't get too excited, and let me explain. During the courtship stage of our relationships, we tend to put our best face on for the one that we have professed our love to. We go out of our way to make them happy and we avoid showing our weaknesses to them. The "in love" experience is when we are getting accustomed to each other's strengths and what we like about each other. The truth is that this phase is mostly a physical, emotional, and/or intellectual attraction in the beginning.

Now here is where I start to get into trouble with many people, but just think about this. When you were dating, ladies, did your husband willingly go shopping with you or do the things that you liked to do? And guys, didn't your wife sit down with you on a Sunday afternoon and watch four quarters of a football game with you, or if you're not much into sports, do something with you that you liked but she didn't really like? I don't know of any couple that can't think of something along those lines. The question is: Why are we like that in the beginning of our relationships, only to watch that start to fade after being together for a while? The answer is a simple one: we have no choice but to eventually allow our weaknesses to show.

For example, most ladies would never go on a date without putting their face on, in fear of their blemishes being visible; or ladies, maybe you're the one who would order a salad for dinner just so you didn't expose the truth that you would rather be eating a full-blown steak dinner. Eventually, you have no choice but to allow him to see you without your makeup and after four or five dates you're starving to death and you finally order a real meal.

For the guys it's the same story; we get new haircuts, put on our best clothes and cologne; we make sure that we are careful to ensure that you get everything that you want even when we hate what you're doing. Eventually, the truth that we love wearing jeans comes out and that we hate shopping or something similar. Loving someone is accepting them for their weaknesses and being "in love" with someone is accepting them for their strengths. The transition from being in love to loving someone is where most relationships begin to waver

The bible talks about love in 1 Corinthians 13:4-7 (The Message) which says:

> *Love never gives up.*
> *Love cares more for others than for self.*
> *Love doesn't want what it doesn't have.*
> *Love doesn't strut,*
> *Doesn't have a swelled head,*
> *Doesn't force itself on others,*
> *Isn't always "me first",*
> *Doesn't fly off the handle,*
> *Doesn't keep score of the sins of others,*
> *Doesn't revel when others grovel,*
> *Takes pleasure in the flowering of truth,*
> *Puts up with anything,*
> *Trusts God always,*
> *Always looks for the best,*
> *Never looks back,*
> *But keeps going to the end.*

Listen carefully to the tone in this passage of the Bible; nowhere does it say that love is when you like what your spouse does or what they can do for you. Actually, the exact opposite is true. To love someone means you'll accept them for everything they are, especially what you don't like about them.

Now let me make an important distinction right now. If there is any form of physical or sexual abuse going on, you need to remove yourself from that situation; sometimes loving someone means leaving them alone and allowing them the opportunity to work on some of their issues.

Moving on, the fact is, in our society today, we are caught up in the WIIFM (what's in it for me) syndrome. We demand from our spouses and others that they love us (accept all of our faults) but we are not required to love them. Now remember I said, love them; not be "in love" with them; which means that we accept them for who they are not, as well as for who they are. The challenge for us is that once it becomes a requirement to love one another, the WIIFM syndrome begins to spread; we put conditions on each other; and the tendency is to start pointing out what we don't like about each other, instead of appreciating what we do like about each other, and loving them for the rest.

Start today to love each other by accepting everything about each other. Once you do, you'll see that you'll start to feel the same way you did when you were dating your spouse and most of us loved life when we were dating. Start dating your spouse again.

Chapter 6

Sex & Love

Sex is another one of those things that is mistaken for love when it is nothing more than a physical interaction between two people. Society says to us that sex feels good and whatever makes us feel good we should love; which translates into, if our spouses make us feel good then we will love them. However, if they don't make us feel good, then we don't love them. This is a setup for absolute failure in your relationship with your spouse; because if you are going to wait for your spouse to make you feel good then you are in for the shock of your life. Guess what your spouse is waiting for from you? You guessed it; they are waiting for you to make them feel good, which has been set in their minds is also the definition of love. So everyone is waiting and no one is doing.

Whatever you do right now, DO NOT mistake what I said; sex IS NOT a bad thing; it is, in fact, a healthy part of a mature relationship. God created us to have an abundant desire, to have sex for a particular reason; we must have babies in order for us to continue our existence. We were built with a purpose of being intimate and having sex is a physical, outwardly expression of our desire for one another. However, sex, as a stand-alone, can never measure up to the requirements of truly loving someone. Now, sex can be an expression of love in the sense that you are saying to your spouse "I love you enough that I am willing to give myself to you physically."

Ultimately, love actually falls in line with an overall theme, presented in the Bible, of the giver or servant. If you look at the explanation in *1 Corinthians* carefully, it refers to the giver more than once; *Love cares more for others than for self; Isn't always "me first"; Love puts up with anything.* These are just a few of the examples that "love" is about being a giver. An even more powerful example comes from God in *John 3:16*, which says: *For God so loved the world that He gave His only son.* He had his son to take the form of man, sent Him to us only to be sacrificed, and He did it all just because He loves us. What an amazing example of true and untarnished love.

You see, love is about sacrificing our needs for the needs of the ones we love. Setting aside our own complaints about what we want from the people closest to us, to give to them what they need from us instead. When we are able to truly walk in love an amazing thing will happen, once this concept gets deep down on the inside. You'll find that the happiness that you are looking for comes from the act of giving, not from getting.

Chapter 7

Marriage: Ownership or Partnership?

We believe that one of the most enduring and longstanding misinterpretations of what marriage should be is the one that says that either the husband or the wife is in control of the relationship; or that because you're married, that gives you the authority to tell them what they can and can't do. Religious beliefs have been formed around the idea that because a woman is not as physically strong as a man, that she shouldn't have any say in what happens, but only does as she is told.

Even in American society today there is this misconception that a man or woman should be able to tell their spouse what they must do. There are plenty of bad examples of marriages being portrayed all over our media today. Daytime television shows exploit the misfortunes of couples, who are struggling to find out the meaning of a good marriage; and we believe that plays into the perception that we have of marriage being one person controlling another.

Just think about some of the nicknames given to married women like *old lady* or *ball and chain*. These terms are demeaning and imply that our wives are like angry old ladies who won't let us do what we want or that they are a weight around our necks that drag us down and make our lives difficult.

Society says that a man who goes out of his way to please his wife is whipped. If going out of my way to make my wife happy, so that she'll want me to be happy, is me being whipped, then I am here to proudly declare that I am the most whipped man on the face of this God-given earth. I am proud to be that man because I can tell you that I am also the happiest man alive and my wife is the happiest woman alive.

American society has it wrong! Marriage is not ownership; it is a partnership with equal shares. Think about this for a moment, if you went into a business with someone who owned equal shares with you, wouldn't you try to work together to make it the best business possible, so that you would both benefit from its returns? Of course you would. Wouldn't you also try to resolve differences in the most efficient and mature manner possible so that you wouldn't disrupt the production of that business? Of course you would. Isn't your marriage more valuable than a business? Then why would we spend more time and energy working at being so compatible with a business partner or a friend than we do with our spouse?

Your spouse is your lifelong partner and they have an equal share in the success of your marriage. Just like you, they want to be happy, they want to feel appreciated, they want to feel loved; and let me let you in on a little secret, deep down they want to be the one that makes you happy too. Realize that you are a TEAM and that stands for: Together Everyone

Accomplishes More. Together, that's what it is all about because it would be an awfully lonely marriage doing everything alone.

Why not be the exception to the rule that says "someone has to be in control of the relationship". Instead, become a partner to your spouse and start doing things that promote the success of your relationship. When you do you'll begin to see a return on your investment that will last a lifetime.

Changing Them Only Changes You

How many times have you thought to yourself, "if they would only start doing this or stop doing that, then I could be happy"?   We really want what's best for our spouse and we express our desire for them to change for the better; however, what tends to happen is that it is received as nagging or complaining.

You have to understand that your opinion of your spouse matters more than anyone else's ;and when you come to them with things that they need to change about themselves, they feel that they are not measuring up to your standards, which is a shot at their self-esteem. Over time that feeling of inadequacy will grow into unhappiness; and when your spouse is unhappy then they will begin to act in a way to make you feel the way they do, because misery loves company. Then when you become as unhappy as they are, you begin to do things to make them feel your pain, and the vicious cycle continues.

So, ultimately the truth is that by trying to change them we only change ourselves and most often make things worse, not better. Listen, not one of us has the expertise to change anything about our spouses; most of the time we find it challenging enough to change ourselves. The fact is that only

God can get people to change and even He can't do it unless that person is willing to change.

Romans 14:1 (Message): Welcome with open arms fellow believers who don't see things the way you do. And don't jump all over them every time they do or say something you don't agree with—even when it seems that they are strong on opinions but weak in the faith department. Remember, they have their own history to deal with. Treat them gently.

In verse 10-12 (Message): So where does that leave you when you criticize a brother? And where does that leave you when you condescend to a sister? I'd say it leaves you looking pretty silly—or worse. Eventually, we're all going to end up kneeling side by side in the place of judgment, facing God. Your critical and condescending ways aren't going to improve your position there one bit.

It is fairly clear that we are to love one another and not to criticize or condemn each other. When we step out of the way and allow God to move in the lives of the ones that we love, then we will have relieved ourselves of the burden of worrying about things that, in the bigger picture, simply don't matter.

At fifteen years old a "friend" handed me my very first cigarette and because of my unhappiness with my circumstances at home I smoked it; from that day on I was hooked. I couldn't get enough of them. It got to a point where I would hang out my bedroom window at night and puff away.

Even in Marine Corps boot camp I found a way to smoke. I couldn't get off of them. At first, it didn't really bother my wife that I smoked, but over time she increasingly would try various ways to "encourage" me to quit. I wanted to make her happy and so I attempted to quit. I tried every quit-smoking remedy that came and I actually did quit for a full year once, but I fell right back into it each time I felt stressed.

My wife was always so disappointed whenever I started smoking again and I ended up disappointing her many more times. However, once we got back into church, within five months I quit I admit I failed one other time after that, but only for a few weeks, and I quit for what I believe to be the final time and I did it with no gum, patch or drug. I did it with God's help. You see, only God can change us or the people we love. We can't change our spouses as much as we would like and as hard as we try to even when we know that what we want them to change is what's best for them. The harder you try to change them, the more they'll resist. I'm sure for those of you who have tried to change someone; you know what we're talking about.

One of my favorite prayers is the serenity prayer which goes like this:

God, grant me the serenity;
To accept the things I cannot change,
Courage to change the things I can,

And the wisdom to know the difference.

We have to learn what we can and can't change, we can work to change ourselves but we can't change anyone else; especially not our spouses and we need to have wisdom enough to understand that truth and pray that God would move in their lives and make the difference that causes them to change once and for all. That's what helped me quit smoking and that is what will help your spouse change.

Chapter 9

The Spouse Lottery

My wife and I are often blessed to have the privilege of speaking with single people who are looking for just the right person; or couples, recently married, who are encountering the differences between themselves. We have noticed a trend that many people are looking to win, or thought they already won, the spouse lottery. What we mean by that is they have built up in their mind what the perfect spouse will look like, act like, and even sound like. Some even have a list of how tall their unfound spouse will be, what color hair, how white their teeth, are and even how much money they make. Some people have it planned out in such detail and they are praying so hard to find the one person in the entire world who will be exactly what they're looking for; they often miss their Mr. /Mrs. Right.

We believe that God does everything to benefit us and that includes giving us a spouse that on the surface seems like everything we asked for and then challenging us to stretch— when we discover that they're not perfect — during the process of becoming one. Think about it; if God gave you a spouse that was, to the letter, exactly what you wanted, and I mean everything right down to every hair on their head in the exact right spot, then how would you learn to handle any adversity in your life when the storms come (and they will come)? We want to encourage you to stop trying to win the spouse lottery and let God do what God does best and match you up with the person that He wants you to be with.

The truth is that most people who play the lottery never win and the ones that bank their future on winning the lottery are most often left with nothing to show for their efforts. Not to mention those who do win the lottery are often not equipped to handle the dramatic change in their lifestyle; and within five years, most of them are in worse condition than they were before. The spouse lottery is no different; and if you are waiting for the spouse who is exactly what you are looking for, then you may just miss your Mr. or Mrs. Right, the one that God has for you.

Proverbs 13:11 (NLT): Wealth from get-rich-quick schemes quickly disappears; wealth from hard work grows over time.

Please don't get us wrong; we're not saying not to ask God to send you the person that your heart desires. We are firm believers that God will give you the desires of your heart; and if that's what you desire, then we believe that God will give it to you. However, it has been our experience that God most often gives us our heart's desire in a package that is not what we were expecting. We must be careful not to miss God's plan for us because we are so focused on the details of what we're looking for in our spouse.

Most likely God will send you the right person who will **become** the person that your heart desires, but won't be that person from Day One. I know some of you are shifting about in your seats right now; but the truth is that God doesn't see things the way we see them, and He most certainly doesn't do things the way we expect Him to. He does things that will not only give us the desires of our hearts but will also mold us so that we can develop into the person that He created us to be.

If you're looking for a spouse, we believe that instead of trying to win the spouse lottery, try trusting that God will place the exact right person, who will fulfill all of your needs and desires, in your path. God will let you know when you found them as long as you're listening to that still, small voice that's inside of you. What you'll most likely find is that the right one is not the one you expected but is the one that God had planned for you.

Before I met my wife I'd given up on trying to find the right woman for me mostly because I was young. I had grown up in a home where my parents mostly fought; and I had been destroyed emotionally by a woman I thought I loved, but in the end cheated on me with more than one person. The bottom line is that I had no intentions of getting involved with anyone; and at the time, I thought it would be that way forever; and honestly I was fine with that.

The U.S. Marine Corps sent me to Guam, which is a very small island in the Pacific. It was exactly what I needed because I

45

was able to get away from everything and everyone from my past and find some freedom. Admittedly, I was just out to have a good time as often as I could. But, this is how good God is; Guam is where I met the woman God sent, to change my life forever – my wife, Marianne. Now on the outside, I looked like everything that she wanted, but I had many underlying issues that she didn't discover until after we were married. I was very bitter and angry because of how I grew up. I had many skeletons in my closets from my past, that over time, she found out; and I was scared of relationships and marriage and all of it.

The fact is I am still wondering why my wife is still with me because she deserves so much better. However, I thank God every single day that she is still my wife because I guarantee that most of you (I'm talking to the women of course), if you were my wife, you'd most likely have tossed me out with the trash. I put my wife through a lot of bad stuff; all that just because I didn't understand how to love someone the right way; but now that I have learned how to love her, she feels blessed having me as her husband. We've been able to grow together and we've overcome so much. We've built our relationship so that nothing and no one could ever come between us.

The bottom line is that no person can come pre-packaged to your exact specifications because spouses are not a possession or a prize. They *are* the best thing that can ever happen to you when you are open to allowing God to fix you up with Mr. or Mrs. Right.

Maybe you are already married, and initially you thought you'd won the lottery, and then felt robbed in someway. You haven't been robbed, but rather you have been blessed by God. He knows what's best for you; and when you begin to trust him and allow God's plan to play out, your spouse will be the one that you have been waiting for your whole life. They will become the spouse you always thought that they were and you'll be one step closer to having a deeper more fulfilling relationship with your spouse; the one that God intended for you to have.

The 3rd Key

Your Mind and Your Mouth Are Powerful – Use Them Wisely

Chapter 10

It Begins with What You Say

What you speak is what you think and what you think is what you believe. What are you saying about yourself, your spouse, and your marriage right now? Are they things that would encourage and make a positive impact on your life or are they things that are negative and destructive?

You can change anything in your life if you simply change what you consistently say about that thing that you want to change; that, in turn, will change what you think about it. And when your mind and your mouth line up, it will change what you believe; and once you believe, all things become possible. The bottom line: How successful your marriage is, is directly related to what you're saying about it.

I think it is very difficult for us to understand the power that words play in our relationships and our self-image. Words can be our most powerful asset and our most difficult challenge. Words can express our deepest feelings and beliefs or be used to mask a truth. Words can inspire, encourage and motivate people to do better, be better, or to achieve more; but they can also be used to demoralize, discourage, or de-motivate a person; convince them that they are nobodies or worthless. Words can make the difference between success and failure, being the best or being mediocre. Words, whether they come from hearing, speaking or thinking, can impact your life and the lives of those you love, dramatically, one way or another.

Proverbs 18:21: (Message) Words kill, words give life; they're either poison or fruit—you choose.

The good news, as this passage points out, is that you can choose what to say; and that will spill into what you believe. There is no rule that says that we must use our words to criticize or be negative. You can choose to use words that give life to your marriage instead. Instead of saying "All you do is work," you could say, "Honey, you're such a good provider and I want to thank you for working so hard for us. I just wanted to tell you that if you did take a break and spend some time with me, I wouldn't hold it against you." If you look closely at the two different approaches, you'll see that one tears down and the other builds up. We always have the choice of what we say. We may want to say something negative to our spouse; but usually when we are saying something negative about them, it is merely a reflection of our inner feelings of pain that are being expressed outwardly.

Matthew 12:34 (NIV): For out of the overflow of the heart the mouth speaks.

The things we say about and to ourselves are as important as breathing and it fulfills the exact same purpose, they kill or give life to our own self -image. If we have a low self-image or if we say negative things about ourselves, then we are killing our spirit and we can't help but to express that image outwardly. It affects everyone around us, especially our spouses, just simply because they are with us more than anyone else.

Far too many of us stand in front of the mirror each morning, looking at ourselves very intently, and say the most negative things about ourselves. Things like, "I need to loose weight," "My hips have grown to the size of a bus," "I'm so ugly," "I don't see how anyone could like me." Anything that you may say to yourself that is negative will only serve to make you believe that your life is not worth what God says its worth.

You don't have to think negatively about yourself because God doesn't create things that are not "good enough" for Him; and when you walk around saying that you're 'a nobody' or you're no good, you're listening to the wrong voice because that's not God. That's the enemy trying to condemn you to a life filled with misery and pain. You can be free from all that by saying to yourself what God says about you.

Even what other people say about you should never affect your own self-image because it doesn't change who God made you. You are a child of the living and one true God of this universe. God has declared you to be the apple of his eye. That means that you are important to God and He loves you, He wants what's best for you. He desires to see you succeed and have an abundance of joy in your marriage. You are not unworthy, you are an over-comer. God has a plan that is bigger than anything you can even imagine and the enemy doesn't want you to fulfill your true destiny. The enemy will send anyone to try to keep you from God's plan for your life.

Philippians 4:8 (Message) Summing it all up, friends, I'd say you'll do best by filling your minds and meditating on things true, noble, reputable, authentic, compelling, gracious—the best, not the worst; the beautiful, not the ugly; things to praise, not things to curse. Put into practice what you learned from me, what you heard and saw and realized. Do that, and God, who makes everything work together, will work you into his most excellent harmonies.

In a nutshell, stop speaking all that negative junk that gets stuck in your mind and start saying things that are positive and good; and God will be able to work through you and bring you to a new place in your life and in your marriage. God is waiting on you to renew your mind before He can move in your life, because He wants to use your testimony to expand His kingdom. Could you just imagine if God were to use someone who always walked around saying "well, I'm just not good enough" or they were always complaining about what's wrong in their lives?

In the same way God wants you to have a joy-filled and abundant marriage. The enemy wants to prevent you from being able to have happiness in your life and he'll do anything to prevent you from living the life God has planned for you. Make no mistake about it, God wants your marriage to be a huge success because if you are satisfied at home, then your children will be happy children; you'll be happier at work, at church, and everywhere you go; God's light will shine through you and minister to people you don't even know. Your marriage becomes a testimony that God can use for His people and your successful marriage helps draw people into Christ.

I say this not to brag on myself but to brag about how good God is. My wife and I often have people come to us, who are either single or have lost a relationship, and ask us to pray for them to find someone, and have a marriage that resembles ours. I've been completely humbled each and every time this happened because I know that we're an ordinary couple, and what they see in us is not us, but God's love through us, and that's what draws them in. Anyone can have a relationship like ours when they stop speaking death into their lives and start speaking life.

I actually first learned about positive thinking when selling funeral services and then carried it on to my insurance career. I was making an incredible amount of money at that time, really more than any twenty year-old man should be making. Life during that time was great; we were happy and care free and I never let anything get to me. Then one day something changed.

My general agent hired a new secretary, and let me just say that she was unique. She and I didn't see eye to eye on much of anything. But instead of reminding myself that I was very happy and making this ridiculous amount of money, I began to focus on what I didn't like about her and I started to complain about this one person. I even went so far as to talk to my general agent and I told him that I would quit if he didn't get rid of her. I'll never forget what he said to me that day; he said "well, at least my life would be happier." You guessed it; now I had something else to complain about and mull over in my mind.

I led myself right down the path to a negative attitude over some relatively minor things that got blown way out of proportion. I eventually allowed it to seep so far into my life that I quit selling for that company, losing the money I was making by trying to show them how much they needed me (a negative attitude also has a lot of pride in it). And all that happened was we had to downgrade our lifestyle because I was no longer making the same amount of money that I had been.

After that I just made one mistake after another over the course of six years. I just got worse and worse; and the worse it got, the more negative I got; until one day I woke up in a state of depression that killed my self-esteem and I felt my life spinning out of control. The feeling of being a failure and my lack of self-anything (esteem, worth, respect) all went down the drain and that led to conflict between my wife and me and all that negative energy spilled over into the lives of our children and it was bad.

It took me years to finally realize that all my failures began when I started thinking negatively instead of staying positive. The very moment I realized what was going on and why things had gotten so twisted up in my life, I immediately put the brakes on my thoughts; and every time a negative thought entered my mind I would stop whatever I was doing and say something out loud that was positive to counter that negative thought. It took significant effort and time to reverse the damage caused by my negative thinking but making that change was the difference. Eventually, I stopped feeling like a failure, my confidence came back, the happiness began to return and I once again felt normal. Then the conflict in our house began to die down and we brought back the positive speaking and thinking.

We started to tell each other what we loved about each other and how much we meant to each other. As long as what we were saying to each other was something positive, we said it. Today, between us we don't have a care in the world. All we know and care about is that we love each other and our children more than life. More importantly, we know that we can overcome anything that life may throw at us.

It all begins with what you say about yourself. Rebuild yourself; start speaking life over yourself and you'll see, over time, a transformation happen right before your eyes.

Chapter 11

Say What You Want To See

You know what happens when two people are speaking and thinking only good things about each other? They become happier people! The way to start focusing your mind on what's positive about anyone or anything in your life is you start telling yourself , **out loud,** to think that way.

I know what you're most likely thinking right about now: "Are they seriously telling me to walk around like some kind of crazy person talking to myself!" Well, the simple answer is "yes." The longer answer is that you are already talking to yourself; but most likely what you are talking about is what is wrong, not what is right in your life. If we look hard enough, most of us can find something good in our lives and talk about those things. Just as important as focusing on what is right, is to speak out in faith the good things that you want to see in your life. Yes, it is amazingly simple but sometimes the simple answer is the correct one.

I learned this technique in my sales career. I would just tell myself that "I can sell anything to anyone" and I repeated that nearly everyday as well as other positive sales statements. At first they weren't necessarily true but it was what I wanted to be true and I kept saying them until they became true. The

Amazing thing was that it actually worked and in just a couple of months I was on the top of the sales charts every single week.

In my marriage it was the same, but different at the same time; because in sales, if someone didn't buy from me, I would just move on to the next one; but in my marriage I couldn't move on to the next wife; so this really had to work. So I started telling myself that my wife was perfect for me, she was beautiful. I would actually tell myself what I loved about how she looked (specific things), that she always takes care of me, and that she loves me, and how she satisfies me in every way. I would tell myself that she makes me a better person and always encourages me, when I was down about anything. I would even tell myself that I loved how she always kept the house clean and how I loved her cooking and on and on and on (I could go on for days). Eventually, I started speaking loud enough for her to hear me, but that's part of the next section.

Does that mean that we never got into any arguments or had fights? No, it doesn't. Does that mean that everything I used to say to myself was 100% true at the time? Most of what I used to tell myself was absolutely true at that time and still is now; but some of what I used to say was more a declaration of faith, than an absolute truth. Is it all true now? Yes! Well, you say, "But Keven, isn't that lying?" No, not lying, it's saying what you WANT to see; in other words, declaring that God is going to change something that we don't have the power, at the time, to change. As a matter of fact, we are instructed to make these declarations in the Bible.

Joel 3:10 (NIV): ...let the weak say, I am strong.

The Word says that it's when we believe that all things become possible. So, if that's true then how are we supposed to make ourselves believe? The only way we have found to do that is to convince yourself to believe; this can be accomplished when you're declaring that something is true even when, at the time, it doesn't seem to be.

You can change anything in your life if you believe you can; and you can believe anything if you tell yourself enough times what you want to believe. (One word of caution, this works the same way when you keep telling yourself negative things also, so be careful what you're telling yourself.) Yes, at first it will feel awkward and strange and you'll have your doubts; but when you begin to say positive things to yourself about your life and what you want to see in your life, you're releasing your faith and allowing God to change what's in your heart, and when what you believe in your heart changes, then anything can happen.

Mark 9:23 (NIV): "What do you mean, 'If I can'?" Jesus asked. "Anything is possible if a person believes."

The definition of "insanity" is to keep doing the same thing over and over again and expecting a different result; so why not do something different for a change. If anything is possible and you're tired of your life the way it is, then why not believe a new life for yourself by changing what you're saying to yourself? Instead of saying "I'm a failure," "I can't do it," start saying to yourself, "I am strong" even when you feel weak; over time you'll feel stronger. Instead of saying "I'm not happy," say, "The joy of the Lord is my strength," "I am loved, I am happy, I am free." The only thing that can happen if you talk better to yourself is you'll start to believe what you're saying to yourself and allow God to show you what He thinks of you. When you see yourself the way that God sees you, then you'll begin to see your chin rise a little higher and you'll stand up taller and you'll begin to express that love, friendship, and appreciation for your spouse and the ones you love. Only good can come from changing how you see yourself to the way God sees you, so why not just do it.

"Well," you say Keven and Marianne, "you just don't understand I was told all my life that I was 'a failure', 'a nobody' or that 'I'm ugly'." Well, I do understand. I too grew up in a home that had no expression of love and I was told my whole life that I would never amount to anything good and I would just end up a failure in life. Marianne was told her whole life that she was ugly and that because she was ugly that no one could ever love her, the way she deserved to be loved.

These are all lies from people who were just so miserable with their own lives that deep down they wanted everyone around them to be as hurt and as miserable as they were. You have to start to understand that the enemy uses even people who are close to us to try to trick us into believing that we are unworthy in some way. Don't be a victim of the lies that are being told about you; give those feelings over to God; rise up and take your life back, by taking control of your mind. Take a stand and don't allow the people who did you wrong to continue to abuse you in your own mind; you can choose what you focus on and you can choose freedom. Let go of that image and start telling yourself that you're worthy, you are good, and that God loves you. Be free today!

Just look at what 1 Corinthians 1: 27-31 says about you: *Take a good look, friends, at who you were when you got called into this life. I don't see many of "the brightest and the best" among you, not many influential, not many from high-society families.* **Isn't it obvious that God deliberately chose men and women that the culture overlooks and exploits and abuses, chose these "nobodies" to expose the hollow pretensions of the "some-bodies"?** *That makes it quite clear that none of you can get by with blowing your own horn before God. Everything that we have—right thinking and right living, a clean slate and a fresh start—comes from God by way of Jesus Christ. That's why we have the saying, "If you're going to blow a horn, blow a trumpet for God."*

God deliberately chose you, the nobody, the failure, the ugly one, the one that everyone counted out, and the one that everyone believed would become just another statistic. He purposely selected you to become somebody. Stop believing the junk that people have told you about yourself, their opinion doesn't count; just listen to what God thinks about you. You're the apple of His eye; you're a child of the King of kings and of the Most High God. You have royal blood flowing through your veins. Instead of saying, "I'm no good," start saying to yourself, "I am chosen by God and He has made me worthy." Instead of saying "no one loves me," replace it with, "God loves me just as I am."

Whenever you are confronted with those negative, self-defeating thoughts just know that God isn't telling you those lies; those lies come from the enemy of God. As soon as those negative thoughts enter into your mind, you need to stop and tell yourself "I no longer have to listen to those lies because I am a child of God and He made me worthy!"

Everyday get up and say what you want to see and then remind yourself what God says about you: "You are the head and not the tail," "You are above only and not beneath," "You are a lender and not a borrower," "You will live and not die." When you say these things long enough and often enough you'll begin to believe it; and once you believe, then God dispatches his angels to go down and stand in the gap for you and you'll see yourself begin to overcome the things in your life that are holding you back. Your words will begin to shift in a heavenly direction and you'll start to see the miracles that you've been praying for come to pass.

Chapter 12

What You Say To Your Spouse Matters

We truly believe that most spouses depend on their mate's opinion of them to help them with their own self-esteem. I'm sure that you'd agree that most of us, when we were dating, wouldn't have continued a relationship with someone who didn't think highly of us. So it stands to reason that one of the challenges that marriages are faced with is a perception (whether valid or not, doesn't change the perception) that your spouse no longer thinks that you see them the way that you used to; and that can (and most likely does) have a significant impact on their opinion of themselves. This perception is created in large part from the things that we say to them, whether what we say comes from our own dislike of ourselves or our attempt to make our spouse better. What we say has just as much to do with how they feel about themselves as what we say about ourselves has to do with how we feel about ourselves.

What we say can also impact how they feel about us. When you say negative things to your spouse long enough, because of the significance they place on your opinion of them, they will inevitably start to resent you for saying those things. The bottom line is that misery loves company; and if your spouse perceives that you are the cause of them feeling miserable, then they will lash out at you to try to make you feel the way they feel. This can only end with one result, everyone is miserable. We can break this cycle by changing what we say to our spouse.

It's easy once you start to see the power that words have in your life and how they change your own self-image, you end up with an amazing realization. If you were to begin to speak positive, life-giving words to your spouse, and you did it long enough and often enough, then their opinion of themselves would get better. Most importantly, their perception that you think highly of them will return and that will help to break the cycle of negativity that may be dominant in the relationship. You see, eventually they will begin to believe what you say about them; and once they believe, God can start to move on their behalf as well.

Remember the things I told myself about my wife in the previous section; well, I started saying them to her and to this very day, nearly everyday, I say to her, "Honey, you're so beautiful, I love how sexy you are," or "I love your 'lips', they are perfect"; or I'll do things like whistle at her when she stands in front of me. I tell her repeatedly that she is the best wife in the world and how she makes me the happiest man in the world.

Well, you may say, "Yeah, that sounds great; but after awhile doesn't she just get tired of you saying the same thing over and over again?" I am here to tell you, that there's not a person that I know on this earth that could ever get too many compliments; it just simply doesn't happen. If anything, it may be a little uncomfortable for you both in the beginning, but after a while you'll think something is wrong with your spouse if you don't hear those nice things they say about you everyday. Once you establish your life giving speech with each other, you open the door for God to come in and start to get rid of the negative things in both your lives. Just imagine the possibilities if God was moving on behalf of both you and your spouse, what could you achieve? What could you overcome? What kind of bond would be between you? My guess would be that you could achieve anything, overcome any obstacle, and create a bond that could last all the way to the finish.

Start today, right now, and start speaking life into your spouse and your marriage. You'll never regret the day that you did.

Chapter 13

Guard Your Mind

We believe we can all agree that the world we live in is mostly negative. The challenge for us positive thinkers (now that you are one), is that to be very careful what we allow into our minds. Staying positive will be the challenge, just simply because we are surrounded by the negative. The news is usually negative, the people we work with are negative, our friends can be, and our family might even be negative. In order to live a rich married life we must (and I mean no other option) guard our minds from as much of the negative as we can.

Romans 12:2 (NIV): Do not conform any longer to the pattern of this world, but be transformed by the renewing of your mind. Then you will be able to test and approve what God's will is— his good, pleasing and perfect will.

What and who you listen to, makes all the difference in being able to maintain a positive attitude. It's hard to maintain when we choose to listen to a bunch of naysayers about how life is so bad and marriage is so hard. Many of the songs we choose to listen to are riddled with tales of divorce and the pain of marriage.

We don't have to listen to the world's idea of what our life should be, they have no idea what a good marriage or a good life is all about. When we choose to listen to or watch positive things and people, it allows us to keep our mind free from the potential of any outside negative influences.

It surprises us how many people get advice from people about something as important as their relationship with their spouse from a friend or relative who has either been married four times or is completely miserable in their own marriage. I know you love your friends; but if they're not providing you with a positive influence, then they can only bring you down; and a true friend would never try to cause you any harm.

But God promised us an abundant life and that includes an abundance of love in our marriages. It's time to detoxify your mind and rid yourself of the enemy's lies for your life and replace it with the truth of God's wisdom. Start saying to the enemy, "I reject your truth and substitute it with God's truth."

Proverbs 16:23 (NLT) from *a wise mind comes wise speech.*

Our mind is part of our treasure; it's the most valuable asset that we possess. Whatever is in our mind is going to reflect in our words and our actions; so it only makes sense that we must focus our mind on things that are good and positive.

You wouldn't purposely sit down in front of your very own computer and begin to load it with viruses, right? Of course not, because you know that it would damage your computer and it wouldn't function in the way it was built to function.

However, often what happens is you're surfing the Internet and you download a file and unwittingly load a virus into your computer. Today, we all have some sort of anti-virus software on our computers, so that the viruses can be caught and destroyed before they can cause any damage; this allows us to keep our computers working properly.

The same is true for our minds; they function even more efficiently than the fastest computer built by man. With sophisticated filing and operating systems, it processes millions of operations each day. The mind is so complex that scientists have yet to fully understand how it works. And yet the simplest truth still remains about our minds. Our minds do whatever we program it to do, whether good or bad.

Proverbs 23:7 (NIV): for as he think within himself, so is he...

You see, if we allow ourselves to watch negative things or we hang around negative people, then we are loading our minds with the equivalent of a virus that can spread into every area of our lives. Left unchecked, it will not only take over our lives but it has the potential of frying our hard drives and making us completely useless. Instead, focus on the positive and guard your mind from the potential viruses that are lurking all around you. When you do that, you can maintain optimum performance and experience richness in your life.

Replacing the negative with the positive is easy. Start by making a list of all the television shows you watch. Is the message in them positive? If not, stop watching those shows; replace it with something that has a positive message; or better yet, use that time to spend with your spouse.

We are firm believers in NOT watching the news reports unless it specifically affects our lives. Yes, we know most people think that you need to know what's going on in the world; but the truth is, the news doesn't tell you what's going on in the world, it merely focuses on the most negative thing it can find and makes it bigger than life. If you watch it long enough you may start to believe that everything in life is bad and that's just not true. The news is not much more than gossip wrapped up in a need-to-know package. If you really, really need to know, replace the TV news with the short version of the news from the radio. We believe that you will hear all you really need to know from that.

Start acquiring motivational CD's from the bookstore or your church. Play them in your car everywhere you drive. Did you know that listening to CD's in your car for one hour a day for three years is the equivalent of a college degree? Think about what your life would look like if you allowed your mind to focus only on things that are positive or that help you gain more knowledge. What have you always wanted to learn how to do? Find a how-to CD and start educating yourself while you're driving; just think of what could happen when you become an expert in that field. It's an amazing thought, isn't it?

We attend Lakewood Church in Houston, TX, and we like to get the CD's from Pastor Joel and listen to them on repeat while we're sleeping. You see your subconscious mind never stops listening and processing information and you can let all that good ,wholesome, positive stuff fill your mind while you sleep, and take hold of your mind and start to change your life.

Some would say, well, you're just brainwashing everyone; well, allow me a moment to be candid; you're already brainwashed to be negative by the things you watch, listen to, and the people you talk to. We believe that most of us need a little positive brainwashing to wash out all of the negative, defeating, and self destructive thoughts that have made our lives difficult up to this point. We want to encourage you, if you're one of those folks who have allowed negativity into your life and it has taken hold, you can take a stand with us and decide to be free from all that junk.

Be bold; let go of those things that promote the negative; begin to renew and refresh your mind by focusing on the positive things in your life; and then you'll begin to see those old mindsets begin to fade away and a fresh, new mindset begin to take hold. You'll begin to win the battle of your mind, and see victory in your life and in your marriage start to rise to the surface, and no one will be able to take that freedom away from you, no matter what happens around you and what people may say about you. You will still be free, you will still be an overcomer and you will live in victory the way God has intended for us all to live. Once you have overcome the battle for your mouth and your mind, you'll be one step closer to having a deeper more fulfilling relationship with your spouse; the one that God intended for you to have.

The 4th Key

Having the Right Priorities

The 4th Key

Having the Right Priorities

Chapter 14

Your Priorities Speak Loudly

Someone emailed this to me and I usually don't pay much attention to these things, but this one caught my eye, largely because it has such a powerful message about our priorities. So many of us use the word 'busy' to describe a situation that it supposed to project an advantage to our spouses and families, but read on; this is powerful.

Satan called a worldwide convention of demons. In his opening address he said:
'We can't keep Christians from going to church.'
'We can't keep them from reading their Bibles and knowing the truth.'
'We can't even keep them from forming an intimate relationship with their Savior.'
'Once they gain that connection with Jesus, our power over them is broken.'
'So let them go to their churches; let them have their covered dish dinners, BUT steal their time, so they don't have time to develop a relationship with Jesus Christ..'
'This is what I want you to do,' said the devil:
'Distract them from gaining hold of their Savior and maintaining that vital connection throughout their day!'
'How shall we do this?' his demons shouted.
'Keep them busy in the non-essentials of life and invent

innumerable schemes to occupy their minds,' he answered.
'Tempt them to spend, spend, spend, and borrow, borrow, borrow.'
'Persuade the wives to go to work for long hours and the husbands to work 6-7 days each week, 10-12 hours a day, so they can afford their empty lifestyles.'
'Keep them from spending time with their children.'
'As their families fragment, soon, their homes will offer no escape from the pressures of work!'
'Over-stimulate their minds so that they cannot hear that still, small voice.'
'Entice them to play the radio or cassette player whenever they drive.'
To keep the TV, VCR, CDs and their PCs going constantly in their home and see to it that every store and restaurant in the world plays non-biblical music constantly'
'This will jam their minds and break that union with Christ.'
'Fill the coffee tables with magazines and newspapers.'
'Pound their minds with the news 24 hours a day.'
'Invade their driving moments with billboards.'
'Flood their mailboxes with junk mail, mail order catalogs, sweepstakes, and every kind of newsletter and promotional offering free products, services and false hopes..'
'Keep skinny, beautiful models on the magazines and TV so their husbands will believe that outward beauty is what's important, and they'll become dissatisfied with their wives. '
'Keep the wives too tired to love their husbands at night.'
'Give them headaches too! '
'If they don't give their husbands the love they need, they will begin to look elsewhere.'
'That will fragment their families quickly!'
'Give them Santa Claus to distract them from teaching their

children the real meaning of Christmas.'
'Give them an Easter bunny so they won't talk about his resurrection and power over sin and death.'
'Even in their recreation, let them be excessive.'
'Have them return from their recreation exhausted.'
'Keep them too busy to go out in nature and reflect on God's creation.
'Send them to amusement parks, sporting events, plays, concerts, and movies instead.'
'Keep them busy, busy, busy!'
'And when they meet for spiritual fellowship, involve them in gossip and small talk so that they leave with troubled consciences.'
'Crowd their lives with so many good causes they have no time to seek power from Jesus.'
'Soon they will be working in their own strength, sacrificing their health and family for the good of the cause.'
'It will work!'
'It will work!'
It was quite a plan!
The demons went eagerly to their assignments causing Christians everywhere to get busier and more rushed, going here and there; having little time for their God or their families; having no time to tell others about the power of Jesus to change lives.
I guess the question is, has the devil been successful in his schemes?
You be the judge!!!!!
Does 'BUSY' mean: B-eing U-nder S-atan's Y-oke?

Being busy for temporary amounts of time is a positive thing, but we must learn to manage our time and keep a balance in our lives. The fact is, that married couples who never see each other are nothing more than roommates and occasional sexual partners (pardon our being blunt). That's not a married life that can last; eventually one or the other or both will wake up one day and realize that they don't even know their spouse and wonder why they're even together.

Think of it this way, when it comes to our jobs or careers, we'll spend whatever time or energy it takes to succeed to get that promotion and we do it in the name of giving our families a better life, but we would suggest to you that your spouse doesn't care nearly as much about having things as they do about having you.

It is true that we all would like to have nice things like a fancy home, a nice car, beautiful furniture, and all the latest gadgets, but what good are all those things if we are always too busy to enjoy them with someone we love? When we spend all of our time working at everything other than our relationship, we are screaming out in our actions that our spouse is less important than whatever we're doing that keeps us so busy.

Early in my career as an insurance salesman I thought it was all about the money and buying new and nice things. I would work whenever I could meet with someone and I would stay as long as it took to make a sale. The company I represented loved me for it and we made great money, but I made that money at a price that I would never be willing to pay today. I didn't really need all the money I made, but I just knew that making money was the key to a successful life and I wanted to make as much as possible. I'm not knocking anyone who makes money because I enjoyed having the money; however, in order for me to always make the money that we had become accustomed to, I worked most of the time. Even when I was home I was buried in the busywork of selling.

Matthew 6:21 (NIV): For where your treasure is, there your heart will be also.

I missed so much time that I could have spent with my wife and my daughter ,Stephanie; and because of that choice, for most of my daughter's early life, it was as if she didn't recognize me, like I was a stranger that just came around every once in a while, and she would avoid me. It broke my heart that she wasn't close to me. Eventually, some circumstances came up that gave me an opportunity to step back and look at my life and my priorities, and make some cold and hard decisions about what was important to me; and I chose my family over my work. To my surprise, I didn't miss the money; and now I don't miss valuable moments with my wife and my children either. What happened, my treasure changed— it went from making money and owning things— to my wife and my children. Changing my treasure changed my heart; in that, I have had much greater happiness and fulfillment in my life, and all without regret.

Ecclesiastes 5:15 (NLT) We all come to the end of our lives as naked and empty-handed as on the day we were born. We can't take our riches with us.

77

The enemy wants us to be so tied up in making money that we can't see the treasure that God has placed right in front of us. Even if we had all the money in the world and the nicest house, car, luxurious boats and every possession that we have ever dreamed that we have ever wanted, we can't even take one single penny with us when we die. So why is it so important to us to amass so many things and have so much money? I used to believe that money was the key to happiness, but what I found out is that my spouse and my children are the key to my happiness. I decided that I want to make my largest investment where I will see the greatest return; and that, my friends, is in the lives of my family; that is what makes me rich, not scurrying around everyday worried about making more money.

Chapter 15

Make a Choice and Stick to It

Whatever we want to be successful at, we will spend the most time on. What we give most of our attention to is a choice not a requirement. If having a successful and rich marriage is something that you want in your life; then you will need to choose to make it a priority and spend the necessary time it takes to make your marriage the richest treasure in your life. The way our life is right now is a reflection of the choices that we have made over the last several years. If you don't have a rich married life right now, then choose to have one from this day on. Don't sit on the fence about it; make the decision and run with it; because if you don't decide, in reality you've made your decision.

James 1:8 (Amplified): [For being as he is] a man of two minds (hesitating, dubious, irresolute), [he is] unstable and unreliable and uncertain about everything [he thinks, feels, decides].

James 1:8 says that the double-minded (people who can't make up their mind) are unstable in all they do. You can never accomplish anything when you're only half committed to it; you need to be all in or all out. When we don't choose to be happy in our relationships, then we've chosen to be unhappy.

Most likely, being unhappy is the opposite of what you want in your marriage.

However, when we are indecisive about what we want from our spouse or when they're indecisive about what they want from us, we'll reach a point where unhappiness has taken over completely and you just feel confused. Then you can't decide how to best handle the situation; or worse, whether you even want to be married anymore. That leads you to pull away from your spouse as a defense mechanism to avoid the feeling of confusion; because when we're confused, we're uncomfortable, and we don't like what makes us feel uncomfortable. In that situation no one can find happiness and everyone is left feeling miserable.

When we're indecisive, we give up any ability to influence any situation that we find ourselves in. It's only by taking a chance and making a decision, whether good or bad, that we find an incredible opportunity to learn and grow. This is especially true when our decision turns out to be a wrong one. We can't learn anything from succeeding, we only learn when we try and fail. Our decisions make the difference (and notice that I did not say our good decisions). Making a mistake is good for us and it produces a positive result because we learn from our mistakes.

Proverbs 24:16 (NIV): for though a righteous man falls seven times, he rises again,

It's not how many times we fall down, but that we get up after every fall. We only need to set aside our fear of making a wrong decision. Make a decision and press forward and when we make a mistake (and some good news is you're not alone, we all will make mistakes), what's important is that we use it to learn from, make adjustments, pick ourselves up, and continue forward.

We don't believe that out of the blue one day we consciously decide to be unhappy, but rather it's something that happens as a direct result of not making a decision to be happy. Think about it, isn't it true that the majority of us start out our marriage similarly by first declaring that we are in love; after some period of time we decide that we have found the person that we want to spend the rest of our lives with because they make us happy; then we take it to the next level and we get married with the idea that we will make each other happy for the rest of our lives?

What does happen is we find out after a year or two of marriage that we have bit off more than we expected, and we have to work at love and marriage. When things get hard we start to wonder that maybe we were wrong and we married the wrong person. Crazy ideas fill our heads and we wonder if the grass may be greener on the other side and then comes confusion. That's the time when we can become indecisive and we begin to see our relationships decline. Some of us even fall into despair because we feel trapped and we lose any hope of ever being happy again.

Happiness is not by chance, it's by choice. You can make a decision to be happy even when it just doesn't seem like you have anything to be happy about. It's when you decide to be happy, even when the world around you is crashing down, that you become happy. Just making a decision to be happy has a strange power to it and you'll be surprised when you start to see the happiness take over your life. It sounds strange but it's true.

My wife and I had been married for only a couple of years and we had reached that point where we started to realize that this marriage stuff takes work and a lot of it. It just seemed like everyday that we were complaining to each other or about each other. We were becoming more and more frustrated with each other which would continually lead to frequent arguments; it just seemed like it would never end.

Then one day we were arguing about something (I don't even remember what it was) and I finally just said enough, and we agreed to separate. I moved in with a friend of mine and proceeded to try to rekindle my single life.

Now the reason that I had allowed it to get this far is so stupid that I almost didn't want to write it down, but I felt convicted to do it even at risk of looking like a complete fool (I'm actually embarrassed right now). The reason was because my wife wanted me to come home after work instead of hanging out with my quote "friends" at the bar after work. Stupid, right? I think it is and it was I who did it.

I was being a complete idiot, but it was also the greatest thing that ever happened in our marriage because when I was alone one day in my friend's apartment (and it was exactly seven days after I had moved out) I had a startling epiphany: I love my wife; and I didn't want to let my own insecurities, fears, and mostly my own self-destructive behavior get in the way of us having the happiest, most loving marriage in the world. In that moment I resolved that I would do anything to get my wife back and make our marriage work, so we could be happy together. I have never dialed a phone number faster in my life than I did that day. I got my wife on the phone; very eagerly, I told her that I needed to talk to her and it was important, and she agreed.

Proverbs 2:11 (NLT) Wise choices will watch over you. Understanding will keep you safe.

Looking back, that was the day that I made the wisest choice I have ever made in my entire life and that day was the day that changed my life and my destiny forever. However, the story isn't quite over yet because you are probably wondering, "What did you talk about?"

Chapter 16

The Listen

Now before I get into what we talked about, I want to tell you that this is an important section of this book because if you're unhappy in your relationship, then you're going to need to have this conversation with your spouse. I will tell you that if you're both in agreement after this talk, you will be well on your way to being richly rewarded for your efforts and having a marriage that is better than you could ever have imagined it to be.

At first, when I got there it was a little nerve-racking because I had everything in my head but I wasn't sure how to get it all out in a way that made sense; my stumbling nearly led to another fight; but once I took a deep breath and calmed myself, we sat down and we just talked. I told her that I realized, in a big way, that I loved her and I wanted to be with her, but that I wasn't happy with the way things were between us. With all the bickering and fighting, I knew she wasn't happy either. I went on to tell her that I didn't think that we could go on that way. I explained to her that I felt that if there was no way that we could be happy together then we should end our marriage because it just doesn't make sense and life is too short to waste it being unhappy all the time. She agreed with that.

Next, we talked about what I believed I needed to be happy and married at the same time. I'm here to tell you that some of the things that I thought I needed were fairly outrageous but nevertheless that's what I believed would make me happy. Then I did something that I had never done before, but I have since realized that it has become the cornerstone of why we have the marriage that we have. I asked her, "What can I do to make you happy?" and then **I listened**. Besides, God gave us two ears and one mouth which was His way of saying to us that we should listen twice as much as we talk.

James 1:19 (NIV): My dear brothers, take note of this: Everyone should be quick to listen, slow to speak and slow to become angry.

Admittedly, her list was much shorter (turns out I'm the needy one), but here is the most important point to this story. We listened to each other for the very first time, to hear what the other had to say. After carefully considering what we both had to say, we made a decision "together" to work at making each other happy, not focus our attention on what the other was doing wrong. What was amazing about that is that, by making a decision to make the other happy, we both ended up being happy. Another critical decision that we made that day was that we would do everything together (yes, that meant that we would never do anything alone, which I'll explain in a later chapter) and, lastly, that we would finish life's race together. The most important point is that we made a choice!

Life is hard enough all by itself, but when a marriage is unhappy and complicated and there is always strife, the burdens of life become almost unbearable. On the other hand, even when life is hard, when you have a happy and loving relationship with your spouse, and they do their best to make you happy, and you do everything you can to make them happy, then your marriage becomes your escape from the hardships of life; that's when you can survive anything that life throws at you. When you have a bad day, you know that you can go home and find joy and happiness, love and encouragement from the only people in life that really matter, your spouse and your children.

If your marriage is not where you want it to be, then sit down together, get rid of any distractions that would keep you from having a real face-to-face talk and ask this simple question: "What can I do to make you happy?" Then instead of talking, do something different, and just listen to what they have to say. There's an amazing power that you gain when you just listen to what your spouse has to tell you. You find out what they need to be happy and it also helps them know that what's going on with them is important to you. When you have that kind of wisdom, you are a truly rich person because that's the key that opens the treasure box of your rich married life.

Even if at first your spouse doesn't do anything to try to make you happy, keep pressing forward because it's been proven that when you hang around a happy person long enough, you will slowly become happy yourself and the same will be true for your spouse.

Just think about this for a moment, when you sit down and decide to be happy, you make yourself more attractive. I know it sounds crazy but let me ask you this, do you like being around your spouse when they're complaining and criticizing you and talking as if everything in their life is so horrible? Of course you don't; you want to be around your spouse when everything is great and they're smiling and laughing and you're having a good time. The best news of all is that you can have that relationship with your spouse. Am I saying that you'll never have an argument again? No, I'm not. What I am saying is that you'll find that your arguments will no longer control your happiness, that they're temporary obstacles that can be overcome.

Happiness is the freedom every marriage doesn't just want, but it needs, and that freedom is a choice. So why not choose to be happy, to make the ones you love happy. Then show them that you have chosen to be happy even if things are difficult. When you do, you'll find a miracle waiting for you and you'll also find another treasure to add to your rich married life.

The 5th Key

Make Your Spouse
Your Best Friend

Chapter 17

Your Best Friend Is Your Spouse

Most of us have that one person in our lives that we know that we can rely on whenever we need anything. Ask yourself, when we need to laugh, who do we turn to? When we want to go somewhere or do something just to get away, who do we call? When we need to bend someone's ear and tell our deepest and most intimate secrets to, who is that person that we tell? Most of us turn to that one person that we call our best friend. It is great to have a best friend, that one person that we want to hang out with and do things with. To have a person who'll listen to every word we have to say just because they're our best friend.

We firmly believe that **every married couple should each have a best friend; however, their best friend should be each other.**

Yes, we know that many of you just had a vision of "they're crazy if they think I'm giving up my best friend" flash before your eyes. Just take a deep breath and hold that thought for just a moment and hear us out. We are not saying that you should disown your current friends (unless they are trying to come between you and your spouse, then you really need to think about it), but rather to change the priority of who your best friend in the whole wide world is, the one who'll be there with you until you leave this life.

Think of it this way, when we first get married we are filled up by the well-wishers, all telling us that they hope that our marriage lasts and that they wish for our love to burn brightly and all those good things that are nearly required to be said at a wedding. Now most well-wishers are our closest family and friends. So if what they said at your wedding is true, and they truly want your marriage to stand the test of time, then it stands to reason that they would understand that your spouse should always come before them.

I was talking with a co-agent I worked with about attending a birthday party for the general agent that we were working for and he asked me if I was going. I very quickly told him "no" and that I was going home to see my wife. Of which he asked me, "You would rather go home, than go out with your friends?" The answer was very matter-of-factly, "yes." The look on his face said it all; he thought I was crazy. I simply explained to him that I don't like to go anywhere without my wife because I would rather be with her.

I could very easily see that this was a confusing subject for him; so I tried to simplify it and told him, "my wife is my best friend and I prefer to be with her than with you." He still thought I was lying to him but he at least admitted that he couldn't argue because he had had four unsuccessful marriages. My guess would be that his misfortune in his relationships had a lot to do with the priorities of his friends over his wife (wives). His wife wasn't his best friend and his best friend kept him from enjoying the happiness of his marriage.

You see the day that my wife and I had "the listen," we made a decision that we would do everything together no matter what it was or how crazy it was (and believe me we did some crazy things), but we did them together. If she wanted to go shopping for hours, I went with her; and when I wanted to go spear fishing all night long, she went. The point wasn't that we wanted to do what the other liked to do, but that we were together, and by always being together our friendship deepened to the best friend's level. But something else happened; our love for each other began to grow at a wild fire's pace. Now, with everyday that goes by, our love for each other gets better and better and we fall deeper and deeper in love. We have never looked back since "the listen" and I can tell you that the love that we have between us today is unbreakable.

It's kind of ironic that most wedding vows say very plainly "forsaking all others." The word "forsake" means to give up, renounce, or sacrifice something that gives us pleasure. We tend to misinterpret that to mean that we avoid only those who may have a romantic interest in us for the sake of our marriage; but we would tell you that not only should you forsake those who have a romantic interest, but to give up spending all of your time with your friends and replace that with spending time with your spouse. All important relationships take time to develop. Spending your time together will allow you to build a best-friend relationship with your spouse. Your spouse as your best friend has significant perks.

So you ask, what are the perks? Just ask yourself, who do you **want** to hang out with? Who do you **want** to talk to? Who do you **want** to ask advice from? Who do you really **want** to tell your troubles to? Isn't it your best friend? You see, when your spouse is your best friend you get to hang out, talk with, get advice from, and tell your troubles to your best friend all the time. Not only that, but you get to be in love and love your best friend, you get to go to bed with and wake up next to the person that you want to be with. There really is no downside to making your spouse your best friend.

Ecclesiastes 4:9-12 (Message): It's better to have a partner than go it alone. Share the work, share the wealth. And if one falls down, the other helps, But if there's no one to help, tough! Two in a bed warm each other. Alone, you shiver all night. By yourself you're unprotected. With a friend you can face the worst.

You see, once you and your spouse become best friends everything becomes a thousand times easier, because we want to be with our best friend. So many marriage help books and systems talk about the importance of communication within a relationship, but we would say to you, that if you and your spouse are best friends, then communication isn't going to be any issue at all. Our best friend wants to listen to what we have to say and we want to listen to what they have to say, making communication much, much easier.

Most other books talk about a need for a date night, but I would tell you that if you and your spouse are best friends then you'll do everything together and having "a date night" turns into a date every night. Other books talk about doing nice things for your spouse, which is a breeze when you're best friends. Think about it, best friends are always more concerned about the other than they are about themselves and doing nice things for each other comes naturally.

Song of Solomon (Message) paints a beautiful and almost exotic picture of what life is like when your lover is your best friend:

In *Chapter 1: Oh, my dear **friend**! You're so beautiful! And your eyes so beautiful—like doves!*

*And you, my dear **lover**—you're so handsome! And the bed we share is like a forest glen. We enjoy a canopy of cedars enclosed by cypresses, fragrant and green.*

In *Chapter 2: Get up, my dear **friend**, fair and beautiful **lover**—come to me! Look around you: Winter is over; the winter rains are over, gone! Spring flowers are in blossom all over. The whole world's a choir—and singing! Spring warblers are filling the forest with sweet arpeggios. Lilacs are exuberantly purple and perfumed, and cherry trees fragrant with blossoms. Oh, get up, dear **friend**, my fair and beautiful **lover**—come to me! Come,* *my shy and modest dove— leave your seclusion, come out in the open. Let me see your face, let me hear your voice. For your voice is soothing and your face is ravishing.*

*In Chapter 4: One look my way and I was hopelessly in love! How beautiful your love, dear, dear **friend**—far more pleasing than a fine, rare wine, your fragrance more exotic than select spices. The kisses of your lips are honey, my love, every syllable you speak a delicacy to savor. Your clothes smell like the wild outdoors, the ozone scent of high mountains. Dear **lover** and **friend**, you're a secret garden, a private and pure fountain. Body and soul, you are paradise, a whole orchard of succulent fruits— Ripe apricots and peaches, oranges and pears; Nut trees and cinnamon, and all scented woods; Mint and lavender, and all herbs aromatic; A garden fountain, sparkling and splashing, fed by spring waters from the Lebanon mountains.*

*In Chapter 5: I went to my garden, dear **friend, best lover**! breathed the sweet fragrance. I ate the fruit and honey, I drank the nectar and wine.*

*"Let me in, dear companion, dearest **friend**, my dove, **consummate lover**! I'm soaked with the dampness of the night, drenched with dew, shivering and cold."*

*In Chapter 6: Dear, dear **friend and lover**, you're as beautiful as Tirzah, city of delights, Lovely as Jerusalem, city of dreams, the ravishing visions of my ecstasy. Your beauty is too much for me—I'm in over my head. I'm not used to this! I can't take it in. Your hair flows and shimmers like a flock of goats in the distance streaming down a hillside in the sunshine. Your* *smile is generous and full— expressive and strong and clean. Your veiled cheeks are soft and radiant.*

Life is seen through completely different eyes when you see your lover (spouse) as your dearest friend. They begin to take on a new purpose in your life and you begin to develop new appreciations for each other. We say this with the best intentions in mind; you can be more to each other than just roommates and occasional sexual partners, you can develop a deep, deep friendship on top of being married that will inject a whole new set of feelings for each other that you've not experienced and can't imagine until you've been best friends.

Let me answer the two burning questions that most people ask. Question #1: Is it easy to become best friends? The method of becoming best friends is easy; however, the practice of becoming best friends is not. What we mean by that is all it takes to become best friends is to spend ALL of your extra time with each other and "do everything together." What we've found is that most people have challenges in this area because they're not sure that the sacrifice they would have to make, of time with their current friends, in order to accomplish this, would be worth it.

We can testify to you today, not from some college book that we read a study from but from our own story and experience that it's not only worth the sacrifice but you'll never find more happiness in life; and your life will never be as rich as it can be if you don't make that sacrifice. Your life, your happiness, and in some cases, your sanity, depend on you taking a step of faith and doing something that is outside your comfort zone by making your spouse your best friend.

Question #2: Will this take a lot of time? The straight answer is "yes," it will take time to get to a point where you are going to see any significant change in your relationship. The truth is that it took time for you to get to the point that you're at right now; and except for the very rare case where God steps in and removes the problem miraculously, it's going to take time to form that deep partnership that can only come from the best-friend relationship that you want.

Proverbs 13:11 (Message) *Easy come, easy go but steady diligence pays off*

Becoming best friends with your spouse will inevitably happen when you have a little faith and make a decision to "do everything together"(Of course you can't go to work with each other but you know what we mean), and don't let anything or anyone stand in the way of developing that bond together. It may take time and it may be a little uncomfortable at first; but gradually your steady diligence will pay off, and in the near future you can be sitting atop a mountain, basking in the sun with your best friend and lover, enjoying your life.

Not only that but you'll have the marriage that God originally intended for us all to have, before Adam and Eve sinned. You can have a marriage of companionship, enriched by harmony, peace, love, and joy. Just imagine what it will be like to live, happy and free from what the world thinks our marriages should be, and to have a marriage that most people will not only look up to, but even become envious because of it.

You may be thinking to yourself, I don't know if we're going to make it. You may say to us, "Keven and Marianne, you just don't know how bad it is for us; we fight all the time; we barely say anything nice to each other; and sex life, you mean, the no sex in life. I think that we're too far gone and I just don't have any hope left."

We understand, because we've been where you are and we're here to tell you that there is hope for you because God wants to bring you out of that dark place that you find yourself in. He wants to help you find the promise that He made to you in *John 10:10 "The thief comes only to steal and kill and destroy; I have come that they may have life, and have it to the full."*

We believe that God wants us to live a life full of joy. A relationship that can only be had by becoming a best friend and lover to our spouse, but the enemy wants us to live a life of regret. We must make a choice of whose plan we will follow for our lives, God's or the enemy's. The choice is ours; and having made the choice to follow a path of joy and not regret, we know that the road ahead may have some bumps in it, but it's the road that leads to the freedom we all deserve, the same freedom that Jesus died on the cross for; and all we have to do is decide that we are willing to take the unpaved road that leads to streets of gold.

Make a concerted effort to become a best friend and lover to your spouse and let God open a door to that feeling of freedom in your life. Don't wait, decide today. When you do you'll be well on your way to having that special relationship with your spouse that you've always wanted and have been praying to God that he would give you.

The 6th Key

Life is in Each Moment, So Live It Well

Chapter 18

Treat Every Moment as if it's Your Last

I recently heard a story about a professor who was only in his mid-forties, had a beautiful wife and three children who were all very young. This professor had contracted a very serious form of cancer which eventually spread into his liver. He was told that he only had six months left to live his life. However, even though his prognosis was grim, at best, and after he and his wife got over the initial impact of the bad news, instead of lying down and waiting for death to come, he and his wife decided to embrace whatever time he had left and to live life and every minute of it to its fullest.

They decided to laugh, even about his cancer, and to spend nearly every possible moment creating memories for his family to remember him by once he was gone. He had a rare opportunity to know that his life is fleeting and he experienced a priority shift in his life from his work to his family. What continued to amaze me further about this story is when I heard that he had given one last lecture and to everyone's surprise, he was outgoing and humorous and seemed as if nothing traumatic had happened to him.

The Professor moved his family to a city close to his wife's family and he began his journey to create as many happy moments for his children to remember as possible, all the while knowing that these memories would be the only thing that his children would have to hold onto once he was gone. He went one step further, and at the encouragement of his wife, he wrote a book filled with the memories of his life, to give his children a way to connect to him when he could no longer be with them. What an amazing way to leave a legacy for your family, a final love letter and a life not wasted because of hardship but embraced and lived until the last possible moment.

If only all of us could find a way to embrace our lives in such a way that would leave loving memories for those we care for the most. What's sad is that so many of us leave a legacy of being a hard worker and a dedicated employee. When our life ends suddenly we missed the chance to say goodbye or I'm sorry; our last words not being what we would have wanted them to be because we thought we had more time. The problem is that we don't even know if what we said to our spouse and our children five minutes ago is that last thing they will ever hear us say, let alone what we may have said to them this morning. Wouldn't it be a tragedy if the last words that the people you love remember you saying are something other than "I love you"? It happens everyday, so don't ever think that it couldn't happen to you.

I know this tragedy personally. Growing up I didn't know my real dad that well because my family was broken by the time I was three or four and we had moved several hundreds of miles away. My brother and I would occasionally go to see my real dad during the summer for a couple of weeks but only for a few times. After my mom remarried, we moved more than fifteen hundred miles away from where my real dad lived and the last time we went on summer vacation to see my real dad was when I was twelve. Some things were said that led my father to try to keep us in California without the courts' permission and my mom had to come to take me and my brother back. He tried to sue for custody and our world was turned upside down. In the end my real dad lost all his visitation rights and my brother and I were not allowed to go and see him again.

I did see my father one more time. I was sixteen years old and at odds with my mom and my step-dad (who I call my dad because he is the one who raised me), so I got in my truck and drove from Oklahoma to California to see my father. I called him and told him I was coming; he even told me not to come but I insisted and went anyway. After driving for a little over two days I arrived at his house only to find out that the reason he didn't want me to come was because he was an alcoholic and prescription drug addict. When I got there he had checked himself into a rehab center.

The problem for me was that I didn't have any money left because I left with only enough money to get to his house (I wasn't a very good planner at age sixteen). My father had sent my uncle to find me and because I had no money and no food and no way to even talk with my father, my uncle convinced me that it would be okay for me to sign my father's name to some of his checks and cash them at the bank because I had to eat and I needed gas to get around. It sounded good to me and of course, being young and in a vulnerable position, I listened to the advice of my uncle. I did go to the hospital to see my dad while I was there but I was only allowed a few minutes. I stayed as long as I could and then headed home.

After my father got out of the hospital, he called me very angry, for taking his money; he even went to the extent of trying to file charges against me. I had to talk to a prosecutor in California and I had to agree to sell my truck and pay the money back and that's exactly what I did; but it left me feeling like my own father, my flesh and blood father, cared more about his money than he did for me and that made me so angry, I severed my relationship with him for good.

My father did try to contact me when he realized he was dying. He sent me letters and had a nurse try to talk me into speaking to him. He even went as far as to offer to fly me to California so he could see me one last time; and in my anger, I refused; and my father died, just as he lived, alone and medicated. It's something that I regret as a son, that I allowed a single event to prevent me from telling my father that I forgave him and allowed him his peace before he died.

The one lesson that I have taken away from that experience is not to allow an offense to keep me from knowing the love that my wife and my children have for me, and that they know that not only do I love them, but they are the most important thing in this life to me; and there is not a single thing more valuable to me than them (For the record, God comes first but my family is a very, very close second).

Psalm 39:4(NIV) tells us exactly how to view our lives: Show me, O LORD, my life's end and the number of my days; let me know how fleeting is my life.

We do not have to wait until we are on our death beds to start to treasure the moments that we have together with our spouses and our family. We can act as if the next moment could be our last; and here's some deep truth for you, the next moment could be the very last moment you have to share with your spouse and your children. We are not guaranteed tomorrow because tomorrow never really comes; the definition of tomorrow is the day after today. The only thing you are guaranteed is that you have this moment, right now, today. You can either waste your life in offense because your spouse didn't say something that you wanted to hear or didn't do something that you thought they should do; or you can embrace life like the Professor and create lasting, impactful and positive memories for you and your loved ones to cherish.

Remember when we are dead our pain is over but the pain for our spouse and our children is just beginning, and it only makes things that much harder for them when the very last thing that was said between you was something in anger. We say this as lovingly as possible, but if you love your spouse and your family, then you'll make absolutely sure that the very last words that you say to them are something they can find comfort in because you never know when those words will be your last.

In the next few chapters we uncover some things that we can do to ensure that we remember that our days are numbered.

Chapter 19

Embrace Your Disagreements

Let's all face the truth head on: we are going to have disagreements with our spouses. Most of us are even going to have some flat-out explosive verbal fights (if you are having physical fights, seek counseling immediately because that crosses a marital line that should not be crossed, period), and we need to embrace those disagreements because it's within our disagreements that we find our harmony. I know it sounds like an oxymoron, but what we've found is that when we're having a disagreement and even very loud disagreements, that is when we are willing to share things that are troubling us that we would otherwise keep to ourselves.

Have you ever had an argument that started out as just a simple disagreement over something, that when you look back on it, almost seemed stupid? And during that argument, were things said that had absolutely nothing to do with the original reason for the argument? My guess would be that we've all seen those days and most likely had plenty of them. The good news is, that it's okay to have arguments like that because it allows us to release those things that are deep down bothering us; and it gives us the opportunity to vent them out. The second advantage to arguing is that it gives us an idea of what our spouse's deepest feelings are; the one's that they are trying to protect you from in a vain effort to avoid upsetting you (We're personally very guilty of this). This gives each of you the opportunity to adjust to the list of "what my spouse needs to be happy" and get rid of those hurt feelings. Of course, making up is always fun too.

In our house we have some rules when we argue and we want to share them with you and tell you why we have them. Rule #1: No one is allowed to go to sleep until the argument is done and we have restored the peace in the house.

Early on in our marriage, when we argued we would just keep going and going and neither one of us would budge from our position. I remember times when we would argue so long that we would literally be dozing off for a few minutes and then wake up a couple minutes later and we kept on arguing, sometimes till daybreak the next day. You are probably thinking that we're crazy, but allow me to explain the reason why, and the advantage of this rule.

Ephesians 4:26 (NIV) ..... Do not let the sun go down on your anger.

You see when you allow "the sun to go down on your anger" or go to sleep angry, what happens is that you wake the next morning with the same anger that you went to sleep with; then one or the other or both of you run off to work not having resolved the conflict. This allows the anger to build and to take root in your life. Allowing that to take root over long periods of time will develop into bitterness towards your spouse; that will, in turn, lead to a communication breakdown and then the real trouble begins. The anger just keeps building and then before you know it, the intimacy will be non-existent; then the unhappiness between you grows like a wildfire and can very quickly get out of control. Basically, you have your marriage in a stranglehold and you are suffocating it to death. One day you wake up and realize that you no longer have a spouse, you just have a roommate.

This may sound dramatic, but folks, it is all too true. We believe that's why nearly fifty percent of all marriages end in divorce. We know that's not what you want from your marriage; you got married to be happy for the rest of your life, right?

It doesn't have to be that way and even if you're already experiencing that level of unhappiness in your marriage, it's not too late to change it. Establish this same rule between you and decide that you'll never go to sleep before any disagreement or argument is resolved completely. Over time you'll find it easier and easier to resolve these conflicts more quickly.

The other benefit is that over time you'll have less and less arguments because you're getting to know each other better, each time you have an argument. After losing sleep a few times you'll both appreciate a quick ending to conflict and you'll find yourselves trying to make peace quickly and get to the making up part.

Matthew 5:9(NIV): Blessed are the peacemakers, for they will be called sons of God.

Although my wife and I still have the occasional conflict between us the most remarkable thing has happened since we began to really focus on how God wants us to be. Most of our energy is spent on making peace instead of proving our points to each other. Today whenever I think I want to argue with my amazing wife, I try to remember this scripture:

Proverbs 20:3(NIV): It is to a man's honor to avoid strife, but every fool is quick to quarrel.

We must all remember that life is fleeting and in the grand scope of things petty differences don't matter. Just imagine the guilt that you may experience if your spouse, the one that you profess to love, were to die suddenly and the very last words between you were in anger. This single tragedy of bad timing would send most of us into a tailspin of depression that would take years, if ever, to recover from that level of guilt. Don't allow yourself to be a victim of circumstance and bad timing.

Rule #2: Whenever we talk on the phone the very last thing we say to each other is, "I Love You." If for any reason we don't hear the other say, "I Love You" and we hang up, we call them right back (I mean within seconds) and make sure that they say, "I love you," to where we can hear it.

Whenever one of us leaves the house we kiss and hug and say to each other, "I Love You." We will periodically call each other out of the blue just to say to each other "I was thinking about you and I wanted to tell you how much I love you." You may say that we're crazy, but the truth is that we are not guaranteed any length of time on this earth; we only have right now, today, this very moment; and I do not want there to be any chance that I would leave this earth without the very last words off my tongue to my spouse being "I Love You."

Not only are conflicts good but we believe that conflicts are part of a healthy marriage as well as part of the process of two becoming one, like the Bible says. You have to keep in mind that none of us are perfect and we are going to struggle with doing the right thing all the time. Don't hate your conflict with each other but rather embrace it—and each other— never allow the sun to go down on your anger and you'll grow to love each other more and create a house that is filled with joy and laughter instead of hate and anger.

Chapter 20

Dance in the Rain When the Storms Come

Doesn't it seem that the harder we fight to rid ourselves of the troubles that we have in this life, the harder we have to fight? For so many of us trouble seems to be our shadow, always lurking and waiting for a chance to cause us to fall. Some of us get so beat down, that we want to curl up in a fetal position and wait for the end to come. Often we wonder why we have to have problems in our lives. We ask God, why can't you just protect us from all the bad things that may happen to us? Why not keep all the storms of life from coming?

The reason that we have all of these problems is not because God hates us or wants us to suffer, but because he loves us and wants us to get stronger and to come up higher. The reason that we have so many difficulties in our marriages is not because God hates marriages; on the contrary, successful marriages are one of the most important relationships God created, so important that he equated His relationship with the church as a marriage.

Revelation 19:7 (NIV): Let us rejoice and be glad and give him glory! For the wedding of the Lamb has come, and his bride has made herself ready.

God knows that the storms will come and he allows them to come for one reason and one reason only; to make us stronger and bring us up higher than we were before.

In May of 2003, my wife and I made a decision to sell everything we owned that could be sold and move from Oahu, Hawaii to Houston, Texas, in hopes of finding a better life. This would be a decision that for a very long time we questioned why we made that choice. What we found, soon after we arrived in Houston, was one of the hardest adversities we have ever had to face. Within just a month of moving, my mother-in-law, who lived with us for the majority of our marriage, was diagnosed with colon cancer and rushed into emergency surgery. After a successful surgery, she was then put on chemotherapy treatment. One month, then two went by, and it seemed as if she was doing well and that over time everything would take care of itself, so we moved on with life.

An opportunity came up during the boom in the housing market and we fulfilled one of our life-long dreams and purchased our very first home. Everything moved so quickly and we signed the papers the day before Thanksgiving; we rushed to move everything so that the very first morning that we woke up in our brand new home would be on Thanksgiving morning. We were so thankful that day, it seemed great.

Our joy was cut short because soon after we moved, the apartment complex that we moved from intended to sue us for moving out because we did not give them a written notice, even though I went to their office and told them I wasn't going to renew the contract, and we were forced to pay them $1,800 (sorry, this is still a little bit of a sore spot for me). Despite this seriously upsetting circumstance, we kept our spirits up and just moved on.

A short while after that we were told by my mother-in-law's doctor that the cancer had spread into her bone and now there was very little that they could do other than to possibly extend her life for a few months with chemotherapy, but there were no guarantees. After a few more weeks of treatment my mother-in-law decided that she didn't want any more treatment. We brought her home and tried to prepare for what was ahead but there is no way to prepare for the death of someone you love.

In the meantime, I was told by the company (I won't mention their name) that I represented that I had to go to a sales manager's conference in Dallas. I was told that even though we were dealing with this situation at home, if I didn't go they would cancel my manager's contract and demote me back to being an agent, which meant two-thirds of my income would be gone overnight, and so I went to Dallas. Almost as soon as I arrived in Dallas, things at home deteriorated and became very serious. The next morning I woke up to a stressful phone call from my wife, her mom's condition was rapidly getting very serious. So, I left the conference without a word and decided to let them fire me. I wasn't thirty minutes drive outside of Dallas when I got a chilling, screaming phone call from my wife that her mom was gone and I wasn't there to comfort my wife and it killed me that I let them blackmail me into going to that conference. The drive home was the longest and hardest three-hour drive of my entire life.

You need to understand the impact this one thing had on not just my wife, but me as well. I loved my mother-in-law like my own mother. She loved me right from the start and treated me as if I was her own son. She showed me what a loving and caring mother was supposed to be and she enriched my life more than I was ever able to enrich hers. For all intents and purposes, and I say this without any disrespect for my mom, my mother-in-law was my mom, and so her passing sent both me and my wife into a tailspin of despair that lasted nearly two years.

Then just when we thought things couldn't get worse, the same people who threatened to fire me finally found an alternative way to get me to resign as a district manager because I was selling a totally different product, that had nothing to do with them, on the side; and in that single moment I lost two-thirds of my income, although I was hopeful at the time that I would be able to quickly make up for it with this other product.

Unfortunately, because of what seemed to be the insurmountable amount of adversity we were faced with, I wasn't able to recover as quickly as I had hoped and we started to fall behind on everything. With that came all the threatening letters, which were more discouraging. We were on the edge of a cliff and the wind behind us felt like it was a hundred miles an hour just trying to push us all the way over.

I had reached a point where I found myself on the floor and no longer wanted to get up. It was so crazy that I had lost all confidence in myself and I felt like I couldn't even sell insurance anymore, which is what I did professionally at the time and had done it for over fifteen years. I remember going to a group presentation and standing in front of just thirty people and my mouth went so dry that my lips stuck to my teeth and when I spoke to this group I just know I must have looked like I was mentally challenged, because I was so afraid that I would fail again.

Our marriage was taking a hit too; with two very depressed people feeling like the world was falling apart around them. We were arguing a lot more than we ever had before. I didn't want to discuss anything about what was going on with me, I just wanted to lock myself in a room and hide from the world. She had reached a point where she no longer felt good enough about herself that she wanted me to love her and it seemed as if the whole world was hell-bent on tearing us apart. Rich married life—ha, ha —we felt like the treasure that we had accumulated all through our marriage had disintegrated into dust and a windstorm was coming.

The truth is I was on my back and I didn't think I could get up again; my wife was not coming out of her depression either. Then something happened one Sunday morning while I was flipping channels on the television. I ran across this guy with a big smile on his face and right as I landed on this channel Pastor Joel Osteen, of Lakewood Church, was saying, "You're a victor and not a victim," and it caught my attention. I watched that whole program that morning and for the next month or so I watched it every Sunday. At first my wife didn't want anything to do with it; but after seeing me watching it so much, she decided to watch it and something happened to her too and I saw just a small spark of life return. The best part of all was that Lakewood Church happened to be in Houston, which is where we had moved to. We decided to go and check it out that next Sunday. The truly remarkable thing is that day we actually had a reason not to go and we almost didn't go; but thank God we went and that's the day we rededicated our lives back to Christ.

Something even more profound happened to us, not right away, but over the course of the first year. We found peace in the raging storm that was our life at the time. Joel Osteen's messages had given me and my wife the glimmer of hope that we had been missing for so long. We found out that the bigger the storm that we can overcome, the bigger the blessing that God has for us. We discovered that the storms are not something to be feared, but something to celebrate and that you can dance in the rain instead of cower under a rock. Did our storm end as soon as we went to Lakewood? No, our adversities were not magically erased as soon as we set foot in Lakewood Church; but I can tell you that we found out that we could give our troubles to God and He would take care of it for us; and it's true; He has done it for us. God always lives up to His promises and we are living proof.

Psalm 34:19 (NIV): A righteous man may have many troubles, but the LORD delivers him from them all;

God is so awesome. Listen, we were on the verge of losing our home to foreclosure, but because of how big God is, the banks that kept trying to foreclose on our home kept making mistake after mistake and for a year and a half (yes, you read it right, a year and a half) they couldn't get it together and take our home away from us. Coincidence? I think not. Then the day came that they finally got it together and put our home in foreclosure. We didn't want to, but after praying about it for days, we felt like we should file a chapter 13 bankruptcy to reorganize and repay all of our debts and it prevented them from taking our home.

Then another devastating blow tried to come and knock us down; the IRS showed up at the bankruptcy hearing and when I looked over at this IRS agent, you could almost see the horns come out of her head and the pure glee that she had on her face when she told me that we owed the IRS $36,000 in back taxes and penalties. My heart just about fell out through my feet and suddenly I was very nauseated. For a short while, I really felt that we had nowhere to turn and that they were going to just come take our home away from us anyway.

Several weeks went by and we came down to the wire, the first payment to the trustee was due and we didn't have the money and we didn't see anyway that we would be able to get the money. So we sat down together and prayed and we told God that we couldn't handle this anymore, this storm looked too big, and we gave it to Him. We clearly told God that we submit to whatever He wanted us to do; and that if He didn't want us to live in our home, that we would sell everything again so we could pay off the IRS and get out from underneath the house payment. We trusted that God would take us wherever we needed to go.

We had two more days to get the money when we started packing our stuff and sorting out what we would keep and what we would sell. I started getting this nagging feeling in my stomach to check the mailbox. I kept trying to put it off but it just wouldn't go away and so I finally gave in and got the mail. I sat down in my office at home and began to sort through it.

Matthew 8:24-26 (Message): Then he got in the boat, his disciples with him. The next thing they knew, they were in a severe storm. Waves were crashing into the boat—and he was sound asleep! They roused him, pleading, "Master, save us! We're going down!"

Jesus reprimanded them. "Why are you such cowards, such faint-hearts?" Then he stood up and told the wind to be silent, the sea to quiet down: "Silence!" The sea became smooth as glass.

MY GOD IS BIGGER THAN THE IRS!! God, at that moment, commanded our storm and told it to be silent. In the mail was a check from the IRS for just over the exact amount that we needed to pay the trustee for the first payment. It turned out that after filing all the paperwork with the IRS that God had rearranged the math and we didn't owe the IRS $36,000; we only owed them $2,800. BUT, this is how great our God is, they owed us just over $7,500 and they had sent us the first of two payments, just in time for us to pay the trustee and keep, not only our home, but everything in it as well. GOD IS GOOD!

God didn't stop there either. On my wife's birthday, she received a phone call offering her a full-time job for a position that she originally didn't feel qualified for and within a few days she got the job, which allowed us to keep up with the monthly payments to our trustee. Then my monthly commission checks started getting higher and higher and today not only have we overcome the challenges of moving from paradise to Houston, we are closer to each other than we have ever been. We love each other more now than we ever have, we rarely argue or fight; all because we found out that we don't have to fear the storms of life but, instead, we can dance in the rain of the storm and give our problems over to God and let Him calm the storm.

Psalm 55: 22 (NIV): Cast your cares on the LORD and he will sustain you; he will never let the righteous fall.

When things in our lives are good, we simply don't get any better or stronger. It is only through our adversities that we become stronger and we learn what we are really made of. Each time we make it through our struggles, it's because God is taking us higher by walking with us through our adversities and helping us to overcome them. In our marriages, adversities should draw us closer together, not tear us apart. It's when we work together, as one, and overcome the trials of life, that our unity gets stronger; then we are more prepared for future storms that may come our way. The more adversity you overcome together, the harder it becomes for the world to pull you apart and the closer the bond becomes between you both. For me and Marianne, we're still standing!

John 16: 31-33 (Message): Jesus answered them, "Do you finally believe? In fact, you're about to make a run for it—saving your own skins and abandoning me. But I'm not abandoned. The Father is with me. I've told you all this so that trusting me, you will be unshakable and assured, deeply at peace. In this godless world you will continue to experience difficulties. But take heart! I've conquered the world."

You don't have to be afraid, you don't have to worry, and you don't have to carry your troubles yourself. When you give them to God and trust that He will not abandon you but He will take care of you, He has you in the palm of his hand. Even better, when you are in the middle of a struggle in life, maybe you lost a job or had to file bankruptcy or maybe you have lost valuable time that you could have spent with each other, don't be upset; instead go ahead and dance in the rain of your storm because God will restore more than was ever taken from you, when you trust Him.

Zechariah 9:12 (Message): And you, because of my blood covenant with you, I'll release your prisoners from their hopeless cells. Come home, hope-filled prisoners! This very day I'm declaring a double bonus — everything you lost returned twice-over!

God is in control and will make sure that you are taken care of. Don't fall victim to the idea that you have trouble because you're no good or that God is punishing you for something you did. No, just the opposite is true; we have trouble to give us the opportunity to come up higher, to get better; so when we weather each storm, we are blessed twice over. The more adversity you have, the higher the position that we receive from God, the better our relationship becomes with our spouse, and the stronger our bond becomes. Remember to dance in the rain when your storm comes because you know that God is going to return double to you for your faith. When you do, you'll be one step closer to having a deeper more fulfilling relationship with your spouse; the one that God intended for you to have.

The 7th Key

The Rich Always Protect Their Wealth

Chapter 21

Protect Your Marriage

Just imagine for a moment that you bought a piece of property out in the country, and one day you were just walking around in your back field and you spotted something glimmering from a small hole in the side of a hill and very suddenly your whole world changed because you found a long-lost treasure on your property. Wouldn't you dig it all up, move it all to a building that may have some kind of security or alarm system? You may even go as far so to buy a guard dog and hire a full-time security guard. The point is, when we have great material wealth, we spend money, time, and energy to protect that wealth.

If it makes sense to us to protect our money and possessions, then wouldn't it also make sense to protect our marriage? We believe that it actually makes more sense to protect your marriage than it does to protect your wealth. We're sure that you'd agree that if you were to come home from work one day and you found your house and everything in it burned to the ground, your first concern would be for your spouse and your children, right? We must make it a priority to always be on guard and be ready to defend that which is most valuable to us.

We believe that most of us want to protect our marriage, but what we envision we must protect it from are things like someone flirting with our spouse. We would suggest to you that you wouldn't have any reason to protect your marriage against things like that if you and your spouse are happy together. What we believe to be the absolute necessities, when it comes to protecting your marriage, are actually things that we do to and for each other. We will discuss these things in the next chapters.

Chapter 22

The Perception of Truth

The truth, what exactly is the truth? Is the truth the same for everyone or do people have different truths? We believe that everyone has a different version of what is true to them because our truth is based on our perspective, which is developed from our individual experiences. Our perceptions actually help to shape the world around us and can help us to stay out of trouble. However, our perceptions can also work against us as well.

In marriage, a negative perception of the truth is one of the single most important aspects that you must protect against. What I mean by that is, let's say for a moment that I was somewhere innocent, and someone had come up to me and out of the blue they gave me the biggest hug, and by accident smudged their makeup on my white shirt and had left the fragrant odor of perfume on my clothes. If I am a man of integrity, that never allows himself to be put in a position of question, then my wife, because of her faith in me and her perception that I am a man of my word, would ask me what happened. When I truthfully explained, she would take me at my word.

However, if I were a man that frequently didn't come home on time after work or was consistently evasive about where I had been or even if I had been caught in a lie about where I was one time, then it is likely that my wife's perception of me would be that I was cheating on her with another woman even if I was telling the God's honest truth. If she believes that I am cheating, then to her, I am, whether it is true or not.

As a married couple we must be vigilant in our efforts to never be put in a questionable situation, no matter where we are or what we're doing. It is imperative that we ask ourselves before we do anything, how our spouse may perceive what we're doing; because unless we are going to walk around with a video camera everywhere we go, it will be based on our word and nothing more.

Proverbs 22:1 (Message): A sterling reputation is better than striking it rich; a gracious spirit is better than money in the bank.

By allowing the wrong perception to creep in on our marriage, we open the door for those little voices, that we all hear when we become suspicious, to start playing, what usually amounts to the worst-case scenario in our spouse's head; and it plays over and over again. Gone unchecked these thoughts will develop into a firm suspicion and eventually a belief that their perception is absolutely true. Once it develops into a belief, you'll find changing your spouse's perception to be an overwhelming task, if not impossible. You must be on guard against even the possibility of the wrong perception being created; and in doing that, you will only strengthen the relationship between you and your spouse.

The things that we have done to avoid creating the wrong perception are:

1. We do everything socially together. If one is invited to a party or get together, if we both can't go, then both of us won't go. Well, you say, that's extreme: It may well be but what's more extreme is to come home and argue all night about something that never even happened because your spouse believes something did happen. Very simply, if they were there with you, then they know what happened.

2. If one of us has to go out of town on any business, every chance we get we call and tell what we are doing, where we are going next, when we'll be done, and most importantly, when we will call them again. The last thing we do before we go to sleep is to call and talk to each other, not for a couple of minutes, but for a long time. You say, "Well even if you do that you could be lying." That's true, but who would go through all of that for a ruse? The more likely scenario, if you were going to be unfaithful, is that you would be evasive and try very hard to end the conversation quickly.

3. We have intentionally become best friends. The fact is most people would not betray a best friend.

4. We tell each other everything no matter how stupid or simple. When you take time to talk even for fifteen minutes about your day and what you've done, even if

it's the same thing you did yesterday, it builds the communication between you.

These are the things that we have done to create a proper perspective between each other and the fact is that none of these things are difficult to do; they only require a small effort and willingness to create the right perception for each other. Just the effort alone speaks volumes about how you love each other and want the best for each other. Once you've created the proper perceptions between you, you will be able to live a more harmonious life together as a couple.

Chapter 23

Pray for Each Other

We believe that as intelligent as we are, being created in God's own image, that we tend to overlook the simplest of things. God created the marriage bond when He created Adam and Eve and we believe He did that as a representation of what His relationship would be with His bride, the church.

Now think about this just for a second. If God created it and the enemy hates everything that God has created, then doesn't it stand to reason that the enemy of God is also an enemy of the unity of marriage? If that makes sense, then doesn't it also make sense that the enemy of God would try to steal what God loves? In John 10:10 the Bible says that the enemy comes ONLY to kill, steal, and destroy. The enemy wants to destroy your marriage to keep you from having the joy that God wants you to have. Very simply, we should stop giving the enemy what he wants and instead give God what He wants, which is for us to have an abundance of love, joy, and peace in our marriages.

For example, most of us like to encourage our spouses in what we believe they could improve on. We want to believe that we're helping our spouses when we do this but the reality is that it will most likely come off as nagging. When you are viewed as nagging, your spouse will react negatively to you and that sets it up for the enemy to come in and steal your joy.

Proverbs 27:15 says (Message): A nagging spouse is like the drip, drip, drip of a leaky faucet; you can't turn it off, and you can't get away from it.

Let me ask it this way, if a man and a woman are united as one, as is described in the Bible very clearly, then the only conclusion that we can come to is that we are part of one other, one part of a whole. If you believe that to be true, like we do, then would you walk around saying to yourself, "You always do this" or "You never do that"? We believe the answer is no, unless you have some much deeper issues.

No, the truth is that we look to our spouse for encouragement and advice, not criticism and condemnation. We're sorry that the truth we are about to say is hard, but it is still the truth. No one wants to be around someone who is a nag; it's that simple. If you nag at your spouse, you open the door for the enemy to step in and play the "Your spouse doesn't appreciate anything you do and all they do is complain" game. Ladies and gentlemen, that is a game that most spouses will play for a while but not for long. We are not saying that you shouldn't encourage your spouse to come up higher and improve in certain areas or you can't ever tell them what they have done wrong, but if pointing out faults to them doesn't seem to work, then a different approach is necessary.

This is really, really important: What we really should be doing is praying for each other every day. If your spouse doesn't want to pray for you, pray for them anyway. God is in total control and He can lead people to change no matter how big the problem is: pray, pray, and then pray some more.

James 5:16-17 (Message): Make this your common practice: Confess your sins to each other and pray for each other so that you can live together whole and healed. The prayer of a person living right with God is something powerful to be reckoned with.

As I mentioned before, for years my wife "encouraged" me to quit smoking and there were many times that I tried. I even quit smoking a time or two but for some reason, it wasn't long after just getting past the struggle of quitting I would find a reason to pick up another cigarette and start all over again. I wanted to make my wife happy but for some reason I couldn't put the cigarettes down for good.

Once we got back into church, we rebuilt our relationship with God. My wife began to silently pray for me that I would quit smoking and to my astonishment one day I suddenly had the urge to quit. I took an herb called Saint John's Wart for two weeks, and put down the cigarette habit, and only fell off the horse one time since then. Today I am tobacco-habit free and I firmly believe that it's for good because my wife prays over me each morning. She prays that God will send His angels down to watch over me and protect me and to keep me from temptation.

Receive this deep down into your spirit: God wants you and your spouse to be happy and to have the desires of your heart and to build up the treasure that is your marriage. The enemy wants to destroy what God has created between you both, steal your joy, and keep you from enjoying the true riches of your marriage. Praying each and every day will serve to remind you that God gave you to each other and it will also establish the boundaries of what the enemy can and can't do in your marriage. Protect your riches: Pray, pray and then pray some more and reap the rewards of a fulfilling marriage.

Chapter 24

Don't Give Temptation a Chance

Matthew 26:41 (NIV): "Watch and pray so that you will not fall into temptation. The spirit is willing, but the body is weak."

Not one of us is perfect (yet) and we're told in the Bible that we'll make mistakes and more importantly that we will be tempted. We believe that because the enemy is trying to kill whatever pleases God that he will mainly try to damage the marital relationship. How he does this is the most conniving, manipulative, and deceptive trick up his sleeve. The enemy steals our joy through offense; when we get offended by our spouse it opens the door and invites temptation into our marriages.

Let me give you an example; whenever I get offended by something my wife says or does (in other words, my pride gets in the way), because I am now a non-smoker, the enemy likes to use smoking to tempt me and starts the mind battle. In order to beat back that temptation I have to rely on my spirit because it's the only part of me that is willing. My flesh screams out to run down and buy a pack of cigarettes and smoke the whole thing. The enemy messes with my mind, telling me all the reasons why it wouldn't matter even if I did just smoke one cigarette. It all sounds good but in my many experiences with quitting smoking, an addict is an addict, and if I were to smoke one it makes it easier to smoke two and then before long I am back to a pack a day.

One of the enemy's favorite tricks is to use the temptation of sex in order to destroy the marital bond. Sex is everywhere you look today; you can find it in magazines, on the Internet, even our favorite TV shows are filled with it; and today you can be driving down the road and up on a billboard you can see a woman or man posing in a seductive manner in order to sell some product or service. The fact is that this temptation is everywhere.

We also must recognize that there are people out there who can sense when we are dissatisfied with our relationships. We believe they are sent by the enemy to try to tempt us into being unfaithful and stealing the joy our marriage brings us. Whenever our marriages are going through difficulties and unrest, you'll likely find one of these temptations lurking around. It's very much to our benefit to avoid unnecessary temptation in an effort to protect our marriage.

The Bible specifically identifies this temptation in Proverbs 5, 6, and 7 and warns that falling victim to this temptation can lead to death. We believe that the death to which it refers is the death of the marital bond. I think everyone would agree, that once a spouse has been unfaithful that marriage is going to be dead, and it would only be by the grace of God that it would be revived again.

The question is how do we guard against this temptation and protect the richness of our marriage? The answer is never use sex as a weapon to punish your spouse for something they have or haven't done. The fact is that all you do when you do that, is invite temptation into their life and the longer there is no sex the easier the temptation becomes (especially for husbands). Remember the flesh is weak and over prolonged periods of time without sex, men have the potential to turn into crazy people who can't think as clearly (no offense guys, but we know it's true), and then we start to reason why we should cheat and how we could get away with it (which of course, most of us don't get away with it because soon after a man cheats he gets a guilty conscience and will likely talk).

Although women don't hold the reputation for cheating, the truth is a percentage of women cheat on their husbands as well. The basic truth is that women who aren't having sex with there husbands are just as tempted to cheat as men are. Sex is a necessary part of the marital relationship and should never be shelved unless both of you agree to it and only for a certain period of time and only if it is for the purpose of getting closer to God.

1 Corinthians 7:3-6 (Message): Sexual drives are strong, but marriage is strong enough to contain them and provide for a balanced and fulfilling sexual life in a world of sexual disorder. The marriage bed must be a place of mutuality—the husband seeking to satisfy his wife, the wife seeking to satisfy her husband. Marriage is not a place to "stand up for your rights." Marriage is a decision to serve the other, whether in bed or out. Abstaining from sex is permissible for a period of time if you both agree to it, and if it's for the purposes of prayer and fasting—but only for such times. Then come back together again. Satan has an ingenious way of tempting us when we least expect it.

This goes back to giving each other what the other needs and you both need sex. It is how God made us and we are not capable of taming the drive for sex within us. We all have the responsibility to keep our eyes on our spouse and remind ourselves that our spouse is all we need and they satisfy us.

Proverbs 5:19 (NIV): A loving doe, a graceful deer— may her breasts satisfy you always, may you ever be captivated by her love.

We believe that by helping each other ward off temptations that often come into our relationships that we can find everything that we never knew we always wanted, and we will have the marriage of an overcomer. When you do you'll have found another treasure to add to your rich married life. We believe with all our hearts that if you have found all of these treasures that we have described, you'll have that richly rewarding, hopelessly in love relationship that you deserve and is an example to a world that is filled with the wrong impressions of what a God led marriage should look like. By doing that we believe and stand in agreement with you that your marriage can and will last a lifetime.

Chapter 25

The Bottom Line

We know that when you follow these keys you'll find out what we did, that you can have that dream marriage that you've always wanted. Just remember the seven keys:

1. Live to give, not to get
2. Get rid of oversized expectations and misconceptions
3. Use your mind and your mouth wisely because they are powerful
4. Having the right priorities
5. Make your spouse your best friend
6. Life is in each moment, so live it well
7. The Rich always protect their wealth

Our deepest desire is for you and your spouse to enjoy a marriage that is fulfilling to you both. We want you to experience the same love, joy, and happiness that Marianne and I share with each other, and we know that you can have that life. In order to become proficient at anything, you must develop your skills and continue to learn. Don't let this book just be a good read one time; read it again in the near future. This isn't the only good book out there related to marriage; read more books and listen to more CD's. The more knowledge you have, the better your life will become so don't stop here, keep going, challenge yourself, and get more knowledge. We know that when you do, you'll continue to grow and you'll continue to add treasure to your rich married life.

Allow us to declare over you both that your marriage has an unbreakable foundation, that, the love you share grows stronger and stronger every day that you are together. When you walk into a room, everyone can see how much love you have for each other. We say that you have an overabundance of love that spills over to the world around you and into the lives of anyone who comes within eyeshot of you.

We declare that you are both givers and not takers, that you have the mind of Christ, and that every word you speak is a word that gives life. We say that no weapon formed against your marriage will ever prosper or succeed, that divorce will never prosper, that any assignment of the enemy to steal, kill, or destroy your marriage is null and void and that the peace of God will reign over your relationship.

Finally, we declare the favor of God in your marriage; we speak joy into your relationship and love that will last a lifetime. God Bless your marriage.

We Love You All,

Keven & Marianne

About The Authors

 Keven & Marianne Card met in Guam on November 2, 1991, where their daughter, Stephanie and their son Branden were born. They currently live in Texas and are about to have another daughter, Izabella. Over the course of their relationship they've developed a relationship overflowing with love and affection. It is because of this that people have often confused them for newlyweds. After recognizing the need that couples have to overcome their challenges and get on a path to freedom and happiness; they decided to write about their experiences, and the secrets they've discovered in their own relationship to lifelong happiness in their debut book, *Forever Newlyweds*. They believe that the return of a morale society begins with the marriage and they've declared it their mission to help marriages succeed. Their prayer is that this book will start a new trend of relationships and marriages that will change the Nation.

LaVergne, TN USA
30 March 2011
222202LV00001B/95/P